W9-CCG-516

HIST Dru
Drury, John. / Corsi, Sandro
The Church In The Age Of Humanism,
From 1300 To 1500.

The Church in the Age of Humanism

An Illustrated History of the Church

Created and Produced by Jaca Book

An outline by chapter can be found on the last two pages of this volume.

The Church in the Age of Humanism

An Illustrated History of the Church

From 1300 to 1500

Translated and adapted by John Drury
Illustrated by Sandro Corsi

J
270
I4
vol. 6

Winston Press   430 Oak Grove   Minneapolis, Minnesota 55403

Los Altos United
Methodist Church Library

2020

Published in Italy under the title
Nasce l'uomo moderno: La chiesa e la sua storia
Copyright © 1980 Jaca Book

**Licensed publisher and distributor
of the English-language edition:**

Winston Press, Inc.
430 Oak Grove
Minneapolis, Minnesota 55403
United States of America

Agents:
Canada—
LeDroit/Novalis-Select
135 Nelson St.
Ottawa, Ontario
Canada   KIN   7R4

Australia, New Zealand, New Guinea, Fiji Islands—
Dove Communications, Pty. Ltd.
203 Darling Road
East Malvern, Victoria   3145
Australia

United Kingdom, Ireland, and South Africa—
Fowler-Wright Books, Ltd.
Burgess St.
Leominster, Herefordshire
England

Created and produced by Jaca Book, Milan
Color selection: Mediolanum Color Separations
Printing: Grafiche Lithos Carugate, Milan

History Consultant: The Rev. Marvin R. O'Connell
                    Professor of History, University of Notre Dame

Winston Staff: Florence Flugaur, Cyril A. Reilly—editorial
               Chris Larson, Keith McCormick—design

Copyright © 1981, English-language edition,
Jaca Book, Milan, Italy. All rights reserved.
Printed in Italy

Library of Congress Catalog Card Number: 79-67835
ISBN: 0–03–056829–3

5 4 3 2 1

An Illustrated History of the Church

The Church in the Age of Humanism

Introduction

The Church in the Age of Humanism describes the fortunes of the Church during the last two centuries of what we call the Middle Ages. These years witnessed the gradual decline of medieval culture, and, at the same time, the struggle of a new culture—the humanist or Renaissance culture—to be born. This period was less dramatic in its challenges to the Church than some earlier and later periods were. There were no Roman persecutions, barbarian invasions or Crusades to contend with, and the Reformation was still in the future.

But the challenges, though perhaps less evident, were very real. New and powerful rulers posed a threat to the Church's independence. The rebirth of commercial capitalism presented unfamiliar and puzzling moral problems in the area of economics. Above all, the Church's internal life grew sluggish and sometimes corrupt; its routine practices seemed unable to foster the lofty ideals of Jesus. Only the saints knew what to do, and—as in every era—there were not enough of them.

Marvin R. O'Connell

1. Europe faced many problems in the 1300s, including the catastrophe of the plague that killed thousands of people between 1348–1350.

Beginning around the year 1300, all the countries of Europe met serious problems that influenced their economic, social, political, and religious life. The most dramatic and frightening event of that century was the catastrophe of the Black Death, or bubonic plague that broke out all over Europe in 1348. This horrible illness was caused by mosquitoes and carried by black rats. Those who became ill were almost certain to die. The plague lasted three years and killed perhaps a third of the people of Europe. For the next two hundred years, European population growth was slower because there were fewer people to have children.

In those country places that had been hard hit by the plague, landowners now had fewer peasants to farm the land for them. In many regions, fields were abandoned and crops were not planted. Because the landowners had less to sell, they became poorer. Some lords tried to change to other crops that would bring in more money, such as flax. Others chose to take almost everything that their peasants produced, leaving the peasants with not enough food for their families. Here and there in Europe, peasants rebelled against these cruel lords, but the peasants had no power or organization, and they were easily defeated.

England and France were at war during this time, and people in the war zone suffered greatly. Villages were looted and crops burned. Between battles, some soldiers formed bands and roamed about the countryside robbing the peasants.

These problems shook up the old order of life in Europe. The rather smooth, orderly way of life under strong rulers during the eleven and twelve hundreds began to break down. New relationships, new ways of doing things, and new patterns of thought and belief began very slowly to take shape among both upper- and lower-class people.

2. During this time,
people's social class
or occupation was shown
by the way they dressed.
Nobles dressed
in their richest clothes
to impress common people.
But all classes faced death
from the terrible plague,
and the "Dance of Death"
was often pictured in art.

At this time—almost seven hundred years ago—it was harder to solve the problems of hunger and disease than it is today. Transportation was poor, and food could not be moved quickly into areas which needed it. Few people understood the causes and treatment of illnesses, and disease was often incurable. The frigid cold of winter brought hardship and death to many.

In food and housing—two of the most basic needs in life—rich and poor people were much alike at this time. Houses were simple, heating was poor, and there was no running water. Food also was simple, and fresh fruits and vegetables were available only during the growing seasons. The rich, of course, could buy more food than the peasants could. And rich people often had a chance to learn to read and to play musical instruments.

One way of telling the poor from the rich was the clothes they wore. At that time, every social class, every rank, and every occupation had its own distinctive dress. Lords and nobles carried their bright weapons, wore their richest clothes, and showed off their family coat of arms when they walked around the city. In fact, all aspects of life were out in the open, for all to see. Lepers went around in groups, sounding their warning rattle so that people would not come near and catch their disease. Beggars gathered outside church doors, showing their misfortunes—such as crippled legs, or ill children—and asked for alms.

To make a good show for the public, weddings, funerals, court trials, and the sale of merchandise were surrounded by processions and banners, grand speeches, and happy or sad singing. After the terrible plague, even Death was represented as a public figure. The "Dance of Death" became a favorite subject in artworks and plays. This art showed a parade of people, each dressed according to his or her occupation or rank in society. Each person was accompanied by his or her future corpse leading the living person on to the dance of the dead.

Medieval cities were surrounded by protecting walls. The church buildings in the cities were the most imposing and important structures, just as they were out in the countryside. People turned to the Church in order to express their faith, their devotion, and their longing for security. Yet they found much to criticize in the behavior of certain churchmen and in the way the Church operated. Faith and loyalty to the Church did not rule out loud grumbling and fierce criticism.

3. From 1300 on, important changes in government took place in western Europe, leading to the formation of strong, centralized powers. In some ways, these new governments threatened the Church.

Over the next few centuries, strong central governments came into existence in almost every region and country of western Europe. In France and England, the ruler was a king. In various German states of the Holy Roman Empire, a princely family held the power to rule. In the republican city-states of Italy, such as Venice, a small group of aristocrats ruled the people.

Northern Italy was a major center of new trends and ideas during the thirteen and fourteen hundreds. In the cities and city-states of that region, several classes of people lived. Noblemen and very wealthy merchants were the "great ones," the *grandi*. After them came the wealthy members of guilds, the members of the "greater arts" or *arti maggiori*. Then came the lesser guilds, and finally the day laborers who belonged to no guild.

The merchants and guild members began to unite to take power away from the nobility. They entrusted government to leaders called "captains of the people." As time went on, these captains became very powerful, kept their power for life, and passed it on to their sons. The cities also hired generals and professional soldiers.

As time went on these new rulers came to have titles such as duke, count, or marquis. Today, we would call them dictators. They were supported by many classes of people, and they hired workers, called civil servants, to keep records, write the laws, and handle the business of government.

For the Church, there were no longer serious dangers from the outside. The Church did not fear persecutions or barbarian invasions such as had taken place in past centuries. But the growth of centralized government and commercial power was a threat. The Church also had to face the question of how to deal with the new interest in ancient Greece and Rome, a pagan culture which emphasized the individual rather than community.

4. Celestine V was elected pope in 1294, but he resigned after a few months in office. Boniface VIII was elected in his place. In 1300, Boniface proclaimed a Holy Year of Jubilee. Thousands of pilgrims came to Rome, but Boniface had quarreled with Europe's kings, and none of them came.

In 1294, a holy hermit named Peter lived on the side of Mount Morone, near Perugia, Italy. Peter was about 72 years old, and he had been a monk since he was 20. Because of his holy life, other hermit-monks came to live under his direction, and he became the leader of a religious order.

In that year—1294—the Church had no pope. The cardinals had been trying to elect a pope for two years, but they could not agree on one person. At last Peter's name was brought up, and all the cardinals agreed that he should be pope. Peter did not want to be pope, but he felt that he could not refuse. He was crowned and took the name Celestine V.

Celestine did not know how to handle the business of the papacy. He agreed to do almost anything and everything that people asked him to do. King Charles of Naples pretended to be his friend, but really used the pope's power to help gain more territory.

Many cardinals wished that they had not elected Celestine, and Celestine himself wanted to give up being pope. One of the cardinals—Cardinal Gaetani—helped Celestine write his resignation. In December, after less than six months as pope, Celestine gave up the papacy.

Almost at once, Cardinal Gaetani was elected pope in December, 1294, and he took the name Boniface VIII. The new pope had Celestine imprisoned in a small cell. Boniface did this to ensure that everyone would recognize him alone as pope. Celestine died in prison in 1296.

Boniface VIII believed that the pope should be a strong, powerful ruler. He believed that the pope had supreme authority on earth in spiritual things, and that he was above all kings and rulers. This was not a new idea about the pope's power. Other popes, especially Innocent III, had believed this. But now times were changing, and strong-minded kings did not intend to let the pope interfere with their rule.

Near the beginning of Boniface's reign as pope, he had a great success. He proclaimed

that the year 1300 was a "Holy Year" or a "Year of Jubilee." This was the first such Holy Year proclaimed in the Christian Church, though the Jews had celebrated years of Jubilee in ancient times.

During the Holy Year of 1300, people could gain a plenary indulgence if they fulfilled certain conditions. They had to make a pilgrimage to Rome, make a full and sincere confession of their sins, and visit the basilicas of St. Peter and St. Paul. The plenary indulgence meant that all the temporal punishment due to them for their sins would be taken away. Later, serious abuses would surround the practice of granting indulgences as they came to be used more and more for making money to pay church expenses. But in 1300 thousands of pilgrims came to Rome from all over Europe. However, none of Europe's kings came to Rome on pilgrimage.

5.
Many Christians tried
to deepen their spiritual lives
with the help of traveling preachers.
Young women began to found
new convents, and an association
of lay women called Béguines
was formed to help the poor and sick.

Between 1300 and 1400, religious fervor deepened. Various groups of Christians everywhere seemed eager to live the Christian life more sincerely. But sometimes these movements departed so far from the traditional teachings of the Church that they were called heretical, or false. Members of such movements often claimed that they were getting back to the true teaching of Jesus, that church officials had gone astray and become too worldly. As a result, church leaders were often suspicious of new spiritual movements. Other movements remained loyal to the Church, even though some of them criticized aspects of church life.

One result of the people's desire for greater holiness was the popularity of penitential preachers. All over western Europe, preachers traveled about, calling people to true conversion and repentance. The preachers urged their listeners to atone for their sins, to give up worldly pleasures and goods as Jesus did. Many people were impressed by their sermons and sincerely tried to lead better lives.

At this time, new convents for women were founded. Many women, especially educated young noblewomen, wanted the Church to teach them how to follow their own way as women toward greater holiness. Franciscans and Dominican friars often took up the task of providing spiritual direction for new convents and for devout women in general. Unfortunately, the spiritual directors often merely imposed the rules and practices of some male congregation without trying to make them fit women's needs.

The Béguines in northern Europe were associations of lay women who took no vows and were not under the rules of any religious order. Béguines usually lived in individual cottages and engaged in charitable works. They went among poor workers and tried to make their lives more comfortable. In the twelfth and early thirteenth century, Béguines were approved by both secular and church authorities. But they were accused of being heretical and immoral, and the force of the movement was undermined. Yet the Béguines have continued to exist down to our own day, mostly in Belgium.

6. Raymond Lull was a scholar and missionary. He tried to unify all knowledge into one system, and he felt that all the truths of Christian faith could be proved to be in harmony with reason.

Raymond Lull was born in Palma, Majorca (an island near Spain) in 1235. He came from a wealthy family, married, and lived a life of ease as a lyric poet and adventurer until he underwent a spiritual conversion. Then he became a Franciscan and devoted himself to theology and all the learning of his day.

In his travels before his conversion Raymond Lull had come to know many Muslims and their religion. He had learned their language well enough to write in Arabic. Raymond wanted Christian missionaries to be trained in the Arabic language and culture so that they could approach Muslims as learned men and preach the gospel message in the

Arabic tongue. He felt that the truths of faith could be defended against the tenets of Arab philosophers, that they could be shown to be in harmony with reason, and indeed that all knowledge could be unified into a single system. His system, known as the *Ars Magna* or Great Art, tried to discover the first principles of all knowledge and unify all learning. Its influence on later thinkers is only now being studied closely by scholars.

Raymond convinced King James of Catalonia (a region in northeastern Spain) to build the College of Miramar. There thirteen Franciscan friars took part in Raymond's program of cultural studies. Raymond wrote theologi-

cal and apologetical works in Catalan, the
language spoken in Catalonia.

But Raymond did not intend to be an arm-
chair missionary. He set out for Tunis, a city
in northern Africa, dressed as a Muslim wise
man. There on the street corners he discussed
the Muslim philosophy and religion with
Muslims and preached the message of Christianity. Within a few weeks he was arrested,
tried, and condemned to death. He was
spared from death and deported, but he returned several times. A pious legend says that
he died of stoning on one of his visits to
Tunis, but he may have died peacefully at
home in 1316.

7. Franciscan and Dominican friars founded communities and hospices in Muslim lands, where travelers, sick people, and pilgrims of many religious beliefs found lodging, care, and protection.

In 1219 Francis of Assisi had preached the Christian message to the sultan of Egypt. His example helped to foster the ideal of spreading the Christian message by preaching and charitable works rather than by the sword. The Franciscans established a house in Palestine, then preached throughout the Near East. Monasteries were built in Jerusalem and Constantinople.

Quick to follow this example, the Dominicans founded monasteries and hospices or guest-houses in Greece and Turkey. Travel-

ers, pilgrims, and sick people found lodging, protection, and tender care there. The monasteries and hospices demonstrated that love and charitable works could help people of different religions and cultures to live together in peace. The mendicant (begging) orders soon moved farther into Asia: to Damascus, Baghdad, Armenia, and Persia (present-day Iran). They preached the gospel message to Muslims and to Christian sects that had cut their ties with the papacy.

These efforts to spread Catholic Christian-ity in Asia were not very successful. But they helped Europeans to feel that Asia was not a totally strange land, that it could be visited and crossed without resorting to armed warfare. So the idea of re-establishing ties with remote Christian sects and of converting non-Christians was revived.

The popes continued sending missioners to the East—to Persia, India, Ceylon (now Sri Lanka), the island of Java, and even to mainland China.

8. In 1303 a serious dispute arose between Pope Boniface and King Philip of France. Boniface thought that he, as pope, had power over earthly rulers. King Philip wanted to be supreme ruler in his land. King Philip's soldiers took the pope prisoner and treated him roughly. Boniface was soon freed, but he died a month later.

During the time that Boniface VIII was pope (1294-1303) several things happened that set the Church and the rulers of kingdoms against each other. For many centuries, the Church had owned the Papal States, a region in Italy around Rome. The pope ruled this area, just as a king ruled his kingdom. This kind of authority is called "temporal" power. Besides having this temporal power to rule a region, the pope was accepted as the supreme religious authority in the West by the Christian rulers of Europe. This was the pope's spiritual power.

Most popes felt that the pope also had some temporal authority over the rulers of Christian kingdoms. They believed that the power of kings and emperors to rule their people depended on the approval of the Church. Pope Boniface, in a famous bull or decree, described the pope's power by saying that the Church controlled two "swords" or powers. The spiritual "sword" was used **by** the Church to help people find salvation. The temporal "sword" was used **for** the Church by rulers who ruled Christian nations under the pope's guidance.

During Boniface's rule, arguments arose between him and the kings of Europe about what came under his authority and what came under theirs. One of the quarrels was about the kings' right to tax bishops and priests. In this case, Boniface had to back down because King Philip of France threatened to punish clergymen who would not pay the taxes. Also, Philip cut off the money that was usually sent to Rome.

A few years later, in 1303, Boniface created a new diocese in France and appointed a bishop who was hostile to King Philip. The king imprisoned the bishop, and a great dispute arose between the king and the pope. Boniface insisted that his power was above the king's, and that the pope had the right to intervene in the affairs of a kingdom if the ruler was wicked. Most of the French nobility and clergy sided with King Philip, and they accused the pope of crimes, including heresy (believing false doctrine) and simony (selling church offices). They wanted to imprison Boniface and put him on trial.

Boniface was in his summer home at Anagni in Italy when he heard about the charges.

He denied them and prepared to excommunicate Philip. Before he could do this, King Philip's troops, helped by some of Boniface's enemies, raided Anagni and took the pope prisoner. Boniface's supporters rescued him in three days, but the 86-year-old pope had been treated roughly and was now in poor health. He died a month later.

The events of Boniface's papacy show that the Church was entering a new era in its relationship with rulers and nations. Many popes after Boniface strove to apply papal power more prudently and to achieve their purposes without violence.

9. Clement V, who became pope
in 1305, was crowned
in Lyons, France.
Instead of going to Rome
to live, he settled
in Avignon, France.
This was the beginning
of the "Avignon papacy."

Boniface's successor, Pope Benedict XI, ruled for only one year. The next pope was Clement V (reigned 1305-1314). He had been the archbishop of Bordeaux, France, and so he was crowned as pope in France, in the city of Lyons. He intended to go to Rome, but he never got there. For four years he moved around southern France, carefully avoiding territory that was under the direct rule of Philip the Fair, King of France.

Clement finally settled in the French city of Avignon. This city belonged to the pope and was not ruled by the King of France. The king was pleased to have the pope in Avignon because then it would be easier to control him.

But the pope wished to remain independent. He had no intention of moving the papal residence to Avignon for good. Several times, he sent word to Rome to prepare for his arrival, but the king pressured him to remain in Avignon.

This was the beginning of the "Avignon papacy"—the 68-year period (1309-1377) when the popes lived in Avignon instead of Rome.

Clement V tried to stop King Philip from going ahead with a trial against the dead pope, Boniface VIII. He was successful, but in return he had to give approval to King Philip, absolve those who had attacked Boniface, and remove Boniface's papal bulls or decrees against France from the official papal records. Besides this, Clement had to agree with the king's request for formal proceedings against the Knights Templar, a monastic order of knights, and eventually Clement abolished that order.

The papal court at Avignon brought in thousands of people: papal officials and servants, cardinals, bishops, visiting delegations, diplomats, lawyers, merchants, artists. Avignon's population grew from 5,000 to 25,000. The papal court was brilliant and busy, but the moral force and example of the papacy grew weaker during that "Babylonian captivity," as the Avignon papacy is often called.

10. Catherine of Siena decided, while still a young girl, to devote her life to God's service. As a member of the Third Order of St. Dominic, she spent her time in prayer and in caring for the sick. A group of followers formed around her, attracted by her personality and her dedicated work.

Catherine of Siena (1347-1380) was the youngest child in the large family of Giacomo and Lapa Benincasa. Catherine was a happy child, and while she was very young, she became devoted to God. As Catherine neared her teens, her parents wanted her to enjoy the social life of Siena and to get married eventually. But Catherine wanted to consecrate herself to God. At the age of twelve she cut off her hair as a sign of her decision to give up worldly life. After some time, Catherine's father supported her decision and at the age of sixteen she was allowed to become a member of the Third Order of St. Dominic. The women of the Third Order followed a Rule, but they were not nuns living in convents. They lived out in the world, giving their time to prayer and to helping others.

Catherine now wore the white dress and black cape of the Dominicans, and she divided her time between the Dominican church, her home, a hospital, and a leprosarium (a place where lepers are cared for).

When Catherine was about twenty, something happened to make her more sure than

ever that she should give her whole life to God. That year on the Tuesday before Lent the people of Siena had a street fair, as they usually did on that day. But Catherine remained in her room, praying. A vision of Jesus and Mary appeared to Catherine. In the vision, she was told that she had an important mission to do for the Church, and that she was wedded to Jesus and his work.

Catherine continued her charitable works and her life of prayer. Her strong, appealing personality and her dedicated religious work attracted other Christians to her. A group of disciples formed around her. They included magistrates, ambassadors, painters, poets, artisans, priests and religious. Though she was young and a woman, Catherine was the true leader of the group from the very start. With these disciples and with the support of the Dominican order, Catherine was free to be very active in the life of her city and her Church.

11. Catherine of Siena
    dictated letters that give us
    a good idea of her
    personality and of her times.
    Catherine wrote
    to all kinds of people—
    kings, popes, poor people,
    invalids—trying always
    to turn their hearts to Jesus.

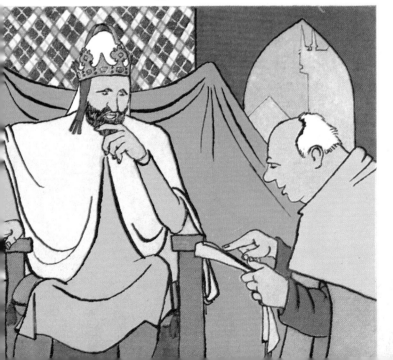

Catherine of Siena was a mystic, an active promoter of charitable works, a spiritual leader, and a diplomat for her city and the Church. Though little educated, she dictated many interesting and well-composed letters to a wide range of people. The letters give us valuable historical information about the times, and they also show us various aspects of Catherine's character and life. Parts of three of her letters are included in this chapter.

Catherine often spoke of the blood Christ shed in his passion and death, seeing it as the symbol of God's life-giving and saving action. She sought to turn all people around her into servants of Jesus, as is shown in this letter she wrote to a bandit leader: "I write to you in the precious blood of Jesus. My desire is to see you a true son and soldier of Christ so that you would be willing, a thousand times over, to give up your life in his service if that were necessary. It would be a fine thing if you would make a serious examination of conscience, if you would consider all the troubles and problems you have brought down upon yourself by placing yourself in the service and pay of the devil. Now my soul wants you to change your way of life, to take up the service and cross of Christ crucified, you and all your followers and companions."

In 1375 Catherine went to the Italian city of Pisa and helped to convert a man condemned to death. Her very human spirituality and her focus on Jesus are shown in this letter she wrote back to her confessor, Raymond of Capua, about her mission: "Dearest Father, I went to visit the man you know about. He was so comforted and consoled that he made a good confession and then made me promise, for the love of God, to be with him on the day of his execution. . . . That day I waited for him at the place of execution, praying all the while. When he arrived . . . he smiled and asked me to make the Sign of the Cross over him. Then he very meekly put his head on the block. His lips uttered nothing but the words Jesus and Catherine. And as he was speaking them, he was beheaded."

In another letter Catherine's bold earnestness is evident. At that time, the pope lived in Avignon, not in Rome. Urging the pope to return to Rome, she wrote: "I, Catherine, servant and slave of the servants of Jesus Christ, tell you to come. Come and do not wait . . . because time will not wait for you. Act like the pierced lamb, whose vicar you are. With no weapons in his hand, he conquered our enemies. His only weapons were virtue and love, his only concern to provide for spiritual things and to restore to humanity the grace it had lost through sin."

12. The Avignon papacy ended in 1377, when Gregory XI moved to Rome. It is thought that Catherine of Siena helped persuade him to come. Catherine's life and work show how love can put new life into the Church.

In 1376, Catherine of Siena went to Avignon to try to help make peace between the cities of Avignon and Florence. While there, she probably spoke with the pope about bringing the papacy back to Rome. For almost seventy years, the popes had been living in Avignon, and many people felt that this was hurting the Church. Catherine had written to the pope, asking him to come to Rome to live.

We do not know how important Catherine's words were, but three months later the pope left for Rome. Upon his arrival there, he was welcomed in great triumph. Catherine was not in Rome when the pope arrived—she had withdrawn to Siena. But she continued to write to him, asking him to help bring peace to Italy.

Catherine continued to work for the Church. She carried out diplomatic missions for Siena and for the papacy. She wrote to all sorts of people, and she was always ready to help settle arguments and disputes. During this time she wrote a spiritual book called today *The Dialogue of St. Catherine*. Catherine was by now thin and often in pain, but her face always had a happy, smiling expression.

Worn out by the intense labors of her active but short life, Catherine grew seriously ill when she was thirty-three years old. Sur-

rounded by some of her faithful followers, she died in Rome in 1380.

Catherine of Siena died without seeing any great change in the state of the Church. At the time of her death, there was still much internal fighting and dissatisfaction. But she and others like her had shown that new life could be injected into the Church through the power of love and good works. Catherine was one of the great saints and historical figures of the fourteenth century, and she has been given the title "Doctor of the Church."

13. Around 1350, Charles IV,
    King of Bohemia,
    established rules
    for electing the emperor,
    and the pope was not one
    of the electors.
    King Charles also asked
    the pope to approve
    a Slavic liturgy—that is,
    a liturgy in the language
    of the Bohemian people.

After the death of Emperor Frederick II in 1250, the German imperial throne was empty for more than twenty years. Then Rudolf of Hapsburg (1218–1291) gained the throne after a long struggle with the king of Bohemia. Rudolf was never actually crowned as emperor, but for many years the house of Hapsburg would be the strongest force in what is now Germany. Also, the Hapsburgs would rule the

region of Austria and its possessions from 1282 to 1916.

Rudolf gave up his claim to the Papal States and lands in southern Italy. He was more interested in claiming lands in eastern Europe and in regaining imperial holdings in German territory that had slipped away while the imperial throne was vacant. The eastward shift of the empire was most clearly shown by the election of Charles IV, the King of Bohemia, as emperor in 1347.

Charles had spent his youthful years in Paris and in Italy. He was sincerely religious. He liked to discuss theological questions; and,

like many other people of his day, he was a passionate collector of relics of the saints.

Social and political life in German lands had been seriously disrupted by the plague and its aftermath. Fanatical preachers were stirring the people up against the Jews, unjustly blaming them for all sorts of problems. Quarrels and wars between regional princes were causing fearful destruction. Charles IV made numerous peace agreements to restore unity to his empire. To eliminate warfare among the princes over the imperial throne, Charles issued the "Golden Bull" in 1356. It decreed that from now on the emperor would

be chosen by seven important officials representing both Church and State.

In Bohemia itself Charles IV was a great and active ruler. He made Prague an illustrious city, and in 1348 he founded the University of Prague, the first university in that part of Europe. He always maintained good relations with the papacy. Charles also saw the need for church reform and spiritual renewal on the personal level. He welcomed reform preachers to Prague, and he obtained the pope's permission to establish an abbey in Prague that would conduct worship in the language of the Bohemian people.

14. In 1378, the Great Western Schism occurred. This schism or split in the Church happened because two and sometimes three men claimed to be pope at the same time.
The problem started after the cardinals elected Pope Urban VI. Later, they claimed that his election was not legal, and they chose another pope, who took the name Clement VII.

Pope Gregory XI died in 1378 and the cardinals met in Rome to elect the new pope. This meeting is called a *conclave* from the Latin words *cum clave,* meaning "with a key," because the apartment or building the cardinals meet in is locked until the election is completed. The conclave of 1378 was the first one held in Rome in seventy-five years because the popes had been living in Avignon, France.

The people of Rome wanted a Roman pope, or at least an Italian one. But they feared that a Frenchman would be elected because eleven of the sixteen cardinals were French.

As the cardinals met in the conclave, a Roman mob gathered and threatened to break into the meetings. The cardinals hurriedly elected an Italian, the Archbishop of Bari, who took the name of Urban VI. Before the election could be announced, the Roman mob broke into the conclave. The cardinals were frightened, but when the Romans learned that they now had an Italian pope, they were satisfied.

Urban seemed to lack the good sense that the leader of the Church should have, and he soon irritated the cardinals by his harsh and haughty manner. Some historians think that Urban suffered from mental illness. At any rate, things grew worse, and thirteen cardinals fled to the city of Anagni. There, in August 1378, they put out a statement in which they claimed that Urban's election was invalid. They said they had chosen him because they were afraid of the mob that had gathered outside the conclave at the time of the election.

In September, these cardinals elected a new pope—a French cardinal named Robert of Geneva—and he took the name Clement VII. Clement tried to regain Rome by force of arms but failed. He then withdrew to Avignon. This was the beginning of the Great Western Schism, or split in the Western Church.

There had been schisms and anti-popes before. Usually, however, they had not created great confusion because it had been clear which one was the anti-pope, and which one was the true pope. But in this case both popes had been elected by the same cardinals. Both Clement and Urban began to act as the legitimate pope, and at their deaths both were succeeded by men elected by the cardinals of their court. Some countries accepted the Avignon pope as the head of the Church, and some accepted the pope in Rome.

The Great Schism lasted from 1378 to 1417, and created a very serious problem in the life of the Church.

**15. Clement VII, one
of the popes during
the time of the Great
Western Schism, gave
permission for the showing
of the "Holy Shroud"
for veneration
by the faithful.
This shroud is a large
linen cloth bearing
the imprint of a human body.
Many people believe that
it had been wrapped
around the dead body
of the crucified Christ.**

The Holy Shroud is a large linen cloth which many people believe was wrapped around the body of the crucified Jesus when he was laid in the tomb. The imprint of a human body can be seen on this cloth. During the Great Western Schism, Pope Clement VII allowed the Holy Shroud to be displayed for veneration by the faithful.

The story of the Holy Shroud is an interesting one. In the Gospels we read that the apostles Peter and John found Jesus' tomb empty, his body gone, and the linen cloths that had been wrapped around his dead body lying there (John 20:3-8). For hundreds of years, nothing more was said about the linen cloths or shroud. Various reasons are given for this long silence. Some people claim that the early Christians preserved the shroud but kept quiet about it. Things that had been in contact with dead bodies were regarded as impure by the Jews, and Christians did not want

to offend them. It is thought that Christians kept the cloth hidden later, during the persecutions, to keep it from falling into pagan hands.

However, in later centuries, the shroud was mentioned from time to time. General references were made to it in the Mass of the Mozarabic rite used by Spanish Christians who lived under Muslim rule. A Spanish bishop in the 600s mentioned in a letter the wrappings from around Jesus' corpse. William of Tyre accompanied the king of Jerusalem on a visit to the emperor in Constantinople in 1171 and reported that the shroud of Christ was venerated in that city. Robert of Clari in his book about the Fourth Crusade reported that the people of Constantinople venerated the shroud and would go to see the image of Jesus' body imprinted on it.

It is thought that the shroud was brought to western Europe by Crusaders and taken to France. There it came into the hands of Geoffrey of Charney around 1354, and the Archbishop of Troyes informed the pope that it was being venerated in the church of Lirey, France.

In 1578 the shroud was taken to Turin, Italy, where it is today. (Because of this, it is sometimes called the Holy Shroud of Turin.) The shroud is displayed from time to time and is venerated by many people. The Church, however, has never declared that this is truly the shroud of Christ. (The Church has never declared the authenticity of any particular relic.)

In the late 1970s, with the Church's cooperation, a team of scientists investigated the shroud. The results of their intensive studies suggest that the shroud may be authentic, but it is not possible to say for certain.

16. At the Council of Constance in 1417, Martin V was elected pope, and he won recognition as the only pope. The Great Western Schism ended. A view of Church government called "conciliarism" gained much support at this time, but was later condemned.

The situation of the Church grew more chaotic as the fourteenth century came to a close. Each of the rival popes created his own cardinals and bishops, and each had his own curia or group of officials. Sometimes bishops and abbots would fight with rival candidates for the same post, each claiming to be the legitimate appointee.

Amid cries for church reform and settlement of the papal problem, the Council of Pisa met in 1409 to try to heal the schism in the Western Church. The Council elected the archbishop of Milan as pope, and he took the name Alexander V, so now there were three "popes" in the Western Church.

During this period another view of church government, known as conciliarism, gained much support. Conciliarism had originally been formulated by canonists (experts in church law) in the twelfth century. In the fourteenth century, scholars at the University of Paris had promoted it, and so had various secular rulers and bishops. Conciliarism holds that the general council exercises supreme authority in the Church. It also holds that all power in the Church resides in the whole body of the faithful; they merely let certain administrators use that power for them. So the administrators must do what the whole body of the faithful want. In short, says conciliarism,

a general council is above the pope, and the council itself governs only through the consent of the faithful.

Conciliarism was basically upheld by the Council of Constance, which met in 1414 under strong urging from Emperor Sigismund. The Council of Constance persuaded the Roman pope (Gregory XII) to resign and deposed the Pisan pope (John XXIII). The third (Benedict XIII) lost all support and later died without resigning his papal claims. Then, in November 1417, the Council elected a new pope who took the name Martin V, and he was accepted by everyone as the true pope. The Great Western Schism was now settled.

Problems of church reform and church leadership remained. The Council of Constance had passed decrees which affirmed the supremacy of general councils over the pope, the collegial role of bishops, a kind of parliamentary government for the Church, and the pope's obligation to hold general councils at regular intervals. Pope Martin V did summon a general council to Pavia five years later, but his successors eventually condemned the principle of conciliarism. Conciliarism no longer had any practical support, even though some still accepted the idea of it.

17. Meister (or "Master") Eckhart, a German Dominican friar, powerfully expressed in his writing and sermons a view of mysticism that stressed God's nearness and the spark of divine life in each person. Eckhart's teachings encouraged Christians to make faith meaningful in their daily lives.

As we have seen, an intense desire for spiritual realities and for a more genuine following of Jesus seemed to take hold of many European Christians from the thirteenth century on. Religious devotion increased in many countries, but it was especially strong in the German-speaking lands of northern Europe. There, many small communities of dedicated Christians arose under the direction of Franciscan and Dominican friars. There, a powerful strain of mystical theology developed to nourish the contemplation and action of sincere Christians.

Words like "mystical" and "mystic" can mean different things. To many people, a mystic is someone—like John of the Cross or Teresa of Avila, for example—who has unusual experiences of God: having a vision of God, hearing God speak, realizing in an exceptionally strong, unforgettable way that God is present, and so on.

Other people say that in some sense every Christian is called to be a mystic. They point

out that the very meaning of being a Christian is that one shares in the "mystery" of Jesus—that is, that one takes part in the "mystical" or divine life that Jesus brings. Hence, they say, every Christian should live in constant union with God through Jesus, and that this is what it means to be a mystic or to live a "mystical" life.

This second view was powerfully expressed by Meister Eckhart (c. 1260–1327), who received his first education in the newly-awakening spiritual atmosphere of Germany. Eckhart became a Dominican and studied in Cologne and Paris. He received the degree in Sacred Theology which permitted him to teach the subject, and hence he came to be known as Meister (or Master) Eckhart. He taught in various schools, held important offices in the Dominican order, served as a spiritual director and preacher to many people, and wrote influential spiritual works as well as theological tracts.

Eckhart stressed the nearness of God to human beings and the existence of a divine spark within them. God is the ground of every human life, he said, and Jesus is present to the human soul. Contemplation and prayer are required if one wants to become a true home for God. Such contemplation, however, should go hand in hand with service to one's fellow humans: "It is well to move out from the delights of absorption in God toward the poor person who claims his soup."

Contemplation in action seemed to be the watchword for Eckhart, and he combined this with an interest in sound intellectual learning which he passed on to his disciples. Some of Eckhart's teachings were condemned. It was felt, for example, that he did not sufficiently distinguish between God and created beings. But the school of mystical theology that he founded was influential in Germany until the time of Martin Luther.

18. Johann Tauler and Henry Suso, Eckhart's disciples, continued to teach his view of mysticism. Tauler was a great preacher, and Suso—also a preacher— expressed his mystical thoughts in poetry. Jan van Ruysbroeck, a friend of Tauler wrote books on mysticism. In England, Dame Julian of Norwich lived and wrote as a mystic and recluse.

Meister Eckhart's teachings inspired two Dominicans who continued his work.

One was Johann Tauler (*c.* 1300–1361), who worked in his native city of Strasbourg. Tauler was a preacher of great influence and power, probably one of the greatest medieval preachers. He became a pupil and disciple of Eckhart, and he was in touch with a popular mystical movement, known as the Friends of God, which spread Eckhart's teachings. Tauler emphasized charity in action and the need to follow the example of Christ.

Henry Suso (*c.* 1295–1366) was another Dominican disciple of Eckhart. At first he favored harsh forms of self-denial and penance, but he gradually came to stress detachment from excessive concern for worldly things. Like Tauler, he defended Eckhart's teachings when some of them were questioned by church authorities. Suso had the flair of the poet, and he presented the Christian mystical view in terms of the courtly-love poetry which was then popular. But he also wrote sermons and a scholarly defense of Eckhart.

Another interesting figure in this mystical tradition was Jan van Ruysbroeck (1293–1381). A priest in Flanders, he retired to a hermitage around the age of fifty and there organized a small community of canons regular living by the rule of St. Augustine. ("Canons regular" were so named because, first, canons were priests who counseled and helped a bishop and who lived near his cathedral. Also, some communities of canons followed an established religious rule or, in Latin, *regula.* Hence they were called canons regular.)

Ruysbroeck's holiness, wise advice, and mystical writings attracted many visitors. He was a friend of Johann Tauler and Gerard Groote, another important preacher of that day. The mystical works of Ruysbroeck, written in Flemish, the local language (not in Latin), are classics of Christian spirituality.

Julian of Norwich (*c.* 1342–*c.* 1423) is another famous person in the mystical tradition. She influenced many people by her counsel and her written work, though she seldom left her home. Dame Julian lived in an anchoress house attached to the church of St. Julian in Norwich, England. (An anchoress is a female hermit who confines herself in a house.) Julian's house was built against the church wall and had a window opening into the church. Here she could speak to people and counsel them. Also, she could take part in Mass. Julian felt deeply the depth and greatness of God's love for people. She expressed her thoughts to those she spoke with and also in her book, *Revelations of Divine Love.*

19. Gerard Groote, strongly
influenced by Ruysbroeck,
gave up his career
as a scholar to offer his
services to the Church.
A group of people who
wished to lead lives
of piety and virtue
gathered around him.
This movement was called
Devotio Moderna, or
the New Devotion.

Gerte de Groote (Gerard Groote) (1340–
1384) lived in the Netherlands. His friend and
spiritual adviser, Jan van Ruysbroeck, deeply
influenced him. He gave up a brilliant career
as a student and scholar, withdrew to a monastery, and was ordained a deacon (but not a
priest). With the permission of the bishop of
Utrecht, he preached repentance and spiritual
renewal to clergy and laity alike. Some clergymen disliked his blunt preaching and had him
silenced for a time.

Groote organized groups of men and wom-
en who lived a community life, seeing themselves as brothers and sisters in Christ. His
movement, which soon spread to other places,
was called the New Devotion (in Latin, *Devotio Moderna*).

Some clergymen were jealous of the devout
life of these lay people; others suspected them
of heresy. So on his deathbed Groote suggest-
ed that members who wished to do so should
join the Augustinian order. In that way they

would be protected by church law. A monastery was founded at Windesheim in 1386, and a convent at Diepenhaven.

But many lay members chose to remain lay people. Called the Brethren of the Common Life, they lived a communal life of prayer, meditation, and literary work. They copied and transcribed the Bible and other religious works. Some became popular lay preachers. Others became outstanding teachers in city schools, despite the group's reputation for being anti-intellectual.

The Imitation of Christ came from the monastic side of this movement. This book eloquently urges people to follow the example of Christ, and it has been perhaps the most popular Christian spiritual work next to the Bible. Today, though, some experts say that it overstresses feelings at the expense of thinking and that it seems to imply everyone should live apart from the world as monks do.

20.
In this and the next three chapters, we read the fictional story of Maurice, an imaginary young workman of Lucca, Italy. This fictional story helps us understand the lives of craftsmen around 1350 and shows the influence of the Church on their lives.

Maurice, the imaginary young man in our story, was the fourth son in a family of farmers who lived near the city of Lucca in central Italy. Lucca had become a free commune in the twelfth century, and then a republic.

At the age of eighteen, Maurice felt that he would have a better chance to earn a good living if he went to work in Lucca. It was a thriving city with many bankers and merchants, and it was famous for its fine velvet and damask cloths.

Maurice went to see Arnulf, the owner of a fabric shop in Lucca. Arnulf's family had originally lived in the same rural area that Maurice's family lived in. In fact, Arnulf's father and Maurice's grandfather had been friends.

When Maurice entered the shop, he was astonished by its size and by the great variety of work going on inside. There were many workers around, weaving and dyeing cloth. The place was more like a small factory than a shop.

Arnulf agreed to give Maurice a job, and he went to work in the dyeing section. The manager, Arnulf, saw that Maurice learned quickly, and he began to teach Maurice the skills of the textile trade. Maurice learned a great deal. For instance, weaving included at least thirty separate tasks. And dyeing the cloth took great skill.

Maurice did not get a salary. He was a learner, or an apprentice. In return for his work, he was taught the trade. The instruction and guidance of a master craftsman such

as Arnulf meant a great deal to Maurice. Some other young men from his home place had come to Lucca at the same time he did, but not all of them were doing well. Some of them had gotten off to a bad start on their jobs. Others did not feel at home in the busy city. Everywhere they went, it seemed, people knew a lot more than they did. They longed for the quiet countryside where they had grown up.

**21. Our story about Maurice
continues. He learned
the crafts of dyeing and
weaving from Arnulf and
eventually became
a member of the textile
manufacturers' guild.
Maurice became familiar
with Lucca, which was
a walled-in city
with its own government
and laws. After about
ten years, Maurice became
the manager of the shop.**

Arnulf, the owner and manager of the textile shop at which Maurice worked, asked Maurice to live at his home with his own family. Arnulf lived near the center of the city, and other textile manufacturers lived in the same neighborhood. Maurice soon got to know them well. Maurice learned the general layout of the city of Lucca, and he began to feel more at home there.

In Lucca, the houses of the wealthier nobles, merchants, and bankers were in the older part of the city, around the cathedral and the bishop's palace. The homes of less wealthy people spread out from there to the old city wall. In years past, as the city grew, people had begun to build houses outside the wall. After some time, another wall had been built around the expanded city.

Merchants and artisans usually had their shops, warehouses, and workrooms near the marketplace. If their work used water, they would build their shops around streams or some man-made water supply. Arnulf's shop was on the shores of a stream because he needed water for his dyes.

The city rulers made laws to control the growth of the city. The streets were laid out according to a plan and were supposed to be wide enough to allow people with loads of goods to make their way through the city. There were laws about how houses could be

built, and laws to prevent people from building homes on public property. The city rulers also tried to keep the squares and marketplace clean.

Shortly after sunset, the gates of the city would be shut and locked. The keys were given to a trustworthy city official until the next morning. Sometimes Lucca was at war with a nearby city, such as the city of Florence, and had to guard against a night raid.

As time went on, Maurice became very skilled in the work of weaving and dyeing. He moved up from apprentice to journeyman, which meant that now he was paid for his work. He took on more and more responsibility, and he joined the guild or association of fabric workers.

One day, about ten years after Maurice had come to Lucca, Arnulf aksed him to become manager of the shop. Arnulf wanted to retire. Maurice, now a master craftsman, could run the shop and teach younger apprentices and journeymen.

22. Now a master craftsman, Maurice longed to share his life with other people. He joined a confraternity, an organization of lay people that did works of charity for the poor, the sick, and anyone who needed help. The confraternity members met two or three times a week to pray together.

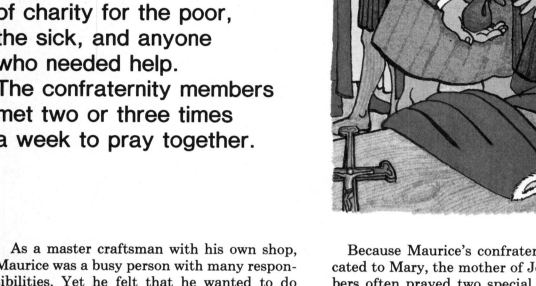

As a master craftsman with his own shop, Maurice was a busy person with many responsibilities. Yet he felt that he wanted to do something to share his life with other people. And he wanted to explore the meaning of life with other people who took God seriously.

Many people of that time felt the same, and often they joined confraternities, or brotherhoods, to pray and do works of charity. Maurice joined a confraternity whose patron saint was Mary, the mother of Jesus. The members met three times a week to pray together. Sometimes they had a meal together in a nearby Dominican convent.

The members and their wives did many works of charity. They offered lodgings in their homes to travelers, cared for the sick, and distributed food and clothes to the needy. The confraternity also tried to help people who had been defrauded in business, robbed, or arrested on false charges.

The people in Maurice's confraternity, as in most confraternities, came from many different social classes and occupations. Some were members of the upper classes; some were artisans and workmen like himself; some were priests or friars.

Because Maurice's confraternity was dedicated to Mary, the mother of Jesus, the members often prayed two special prayers in her honor: the Rosary, and the Angelus.

The Rosary took its name from the Latin *rosarium,* or "rose garden." This prayer is made up of 150 Hail Marys, the prayer based on the words of the angel to Mary at the announcement of Jesus' coming. God's plan for salvation and the life of Jesus are the main ideas on which people meditate as they pray the Rosary. The rosary began as a substitute for the 150 psalms. The educated monks read from their psalter, or book of psalms, and the common people who could not read prayed 150 Hail Marys. For this reason, the rosary was sometimes called "Our Lady's Psalter." The Hail Marys were counted on beads, and from this came the string of rosary beads still used today.

The Angelus got its name from the first word of the prayer in Latin, *Angelus Domini nuntiavit Mariae* ("The angel of the Lord announced to Mary . . ."). The Angelus was prayed at dawn, midday, and sunset. It, too, emphasized Jesus and his saving work.

23. Our story of Maurice
ends with a description
of a feast-day celebration.
In the morning, Maurice
marched in a procession
with his confraternity.
That afternoon, he took part
in a mystery play
put on by his guild
about the death of Christ.

In the spring of 1365, Maurice took part in the celebration of the feast of Corpus Christi. The words *Corpus Christi* mean "body of Christ," and this holy day celebrates the institution of the sacrament of the Eucharist by Jesus at the Last Supper.

In Lucca, the celebration began with Mass in the cathedral; after Mass an outdoor procession was held. (Outdoor processions were often part of holyday celebrations during this time.) The members of confraternities and guilds walked together through the streets, carrying banners and statues, sometimes playing music. Other people watched from the windows, balconies, or along the sides of the streets.

Maurice went to Mass in the cathedral with the other members of his confraternity. In his homily, the bishop told them that the Eucha-

rist was a sign of Jesus' presence among his
people. Just as the bread and wine of the Eucharist brought the faithful together in unity
and peace, he said, so should they live in
peace and unity with each other in their daily
lives.

At the end of the Mass the procession began. Maurice walked with his confraternity in
the procession, and that afternoon he joined
his guild to take part in a mystery play.

Mystery plays and miracle plays developed
in Europe between the years 900 and 1500. A
"mystery play" was not a story about crime
and detectives, but a play about the life (or
"mysteries") of Jesus. Often the mystery play
was put on in several parts, and different
guilds would be responsible for individual
acts. They had to get the props—things needed to put on the play—act out the parts, and

so forth. The plays had been written and put
on in Latin, but now they were often put on in
the spoken language of the people. "Miracle
plays" were usually about the saints and the
miraculous deeds of their lives.

These mystery and miracle plays were especially popular during the 1400s. Many people could not read, and the plays helped teach
them important stories from the Bible.

On this particular day, Maurice's guild of
fabric manufacturers was responsible for the
part or act of the mystery play that showed
Jesus' passion and death. After the procession
they performed their play in a market near
the city. Then they went to another part of
the city and put the play on again, so that
other people could see it. Other guilds did the
same with their plays.

24. Around the year 1400, European cities grew in number and in population. Many cities were important centers of business and political power. In some cities, and most noticeably in Italy, humanism and the arts were growing stronger.

Political, economic, and social life in Europe became more lively and varied in the fifteenth century. Wars, popular revolts, and situations of dire want continued, but there were signs of revival.

Europe's population had decreased, largely because of the plague. Now a larger percentage of people lived in cities, even though agriculture and rural life still predominated. The big cathedral cities (shown on the map) continued to be very important, but other cities, such as London in England and Barcelona in Spain, were also important as centers of business activity.

In the cities, new business techniques, such as letters of credit and using currency instead of barter, helped the rapid growth of active commerce. While the cities sheltered many poor laborers and refugees from the countryside, they could also boast of wealthy merchant families and high churchmen who lived lavishly and indulged in luxury goods imported from foreign lands. Artisans of great technical skill were improving their crafts and, in some cases, developing into truly great artists. Philosophers in the scholastic tradition were beginning to explore issues that would become central concerns of modern science. Some humanists were beginning to learn classical Greek so that they could read the ancient works of Greeks and Romans. In these ancient writings, humanists tried to find a better way of understanding the universe and ruling themselves. From Italy these trends would gradually spread to northern and western Europe, though each area had its own distinctive seeds of development.

There were signs of revival in the countryside as well. Sheep-raising became important in parts of England, Spain, and Italy as the wool industry continued to grow in importance, but farming also recovered in many areas. Ravaged farmlands and marshy areas were reclaimed. Peasants were often invited to new areas to undertake this work, and the terms were rather favorable to them because there was a shortage of people. For example, the whole harvest might be divided equally between landowner and peasant; and a low fixed rent might replace all the older forms of peasant-lord obligations.

Commerce and trade was very active. Luxury goods came from the East, though some quality things were now being manufactured in Italian cities as well. Basic foodstuffs, grain, wood, and mining products were shipped along the rivers of Europe as well as along the Mediterranean and Baltic coasts. The Mediterranean area remained the center of trade and commerce, and Italy was the economic and artistic hub of Europe.

25. During the 1300s and 1400s Islamic Turks conquered Serbia, Bulgaria, and parts of Greece. The Byzantine empire lost everything but the city of Constantinople and the region around it.

From the close of the thirteenth century on, a new political and military force had been building up in the Near East. This force was the Ottoman Turks, a nation of fierce raiders who had developed a strong military organization. The Turks had given up their old tribal religion and were now Muslims. Their military ability, their enthusiasm, and their strong organization made them a terrifying opponent as they swept towards the Balkans.

The first kingdom there to fall to the Turks was Serbia. By the fourteenth century Serbia had become a powerful kingdom in the central Balkans, but the Turks crushed an army of noblemen at the battle of Kossovo in 1389.

Turkish successes continued. In 1393 the Turks conquered Bulgaria and parts of Greece. The Byzantine empire was reduced to a few patches of territory around its capital, Constantinople. And that city would fall to them in 1453, as we shall see in a later chapter.

The advance of the Ottoman Turks was now beginning to affect Christian countries faithful to the Roman Church. North of Serbia lay the kingdom of Hungary, whose ties with Rome went back to King Stephen of Hungary and the eleventh century. For decades, the Hungarians would courageously fight bloody battles against the Turks.

The high point of this particular Turkish thrust into Europe was the siege of Belgrade. At this time the city was part of the kingdom

of Hungary, and its fortress guarded the entrance to the fertile plains of Hungary and central Europe. In 1456, Belgrade was threatened by a Turkish army of 100,000 men. John Hunyadi, a Hungarian nobleman who had already won some victories over the Turks, moved to the defense of the city with a much smaller army. He was joined, however, by the 20,000 Crusaders who had been recruited by John Capistran and other Franciscans in Hungary, with the help and encouragement of Pope Calixtus III. When the Turks attacked, the combined Christian forces drove them back and won the day. The Turkish conquest of Hungary was put off till 1526—some seventy years.

Albanian tribesmen also put up fierce resistance to the Turks. But Iskander Bey (George Scanderbeg) and some other powerful leaders died, and the Crusaders quarreled among themselves and finally gave up the Crusade. So Albania fell to the Turks, who took over the land. Under Turkish rule, Albanian Christians lost their rights to property and were forbidden to get an education or enter the professions, such as medicine and teaching.

26. John Wycliffe, a fourteenth-century English scholar, criticized abuses in the Church. Wycliffe loved the Bible and thought that it was all that was needed for moral teaching and faith.

A number of popular protests arose in the 1300s because some clergymen were too worldly, because church leaders failed to reform the Church, and because during the Great Western Schism people could not even be sure who was the real pope.

Many loyal Christians were angry about abuses in the Church and wanted to reform it, but they had no intention of leaving the Church. Others, though, were rethinking their religious heritage and reaching conclusions that were different from standard beliefs and practices.

One leader in such thinking was John Wycliffe (c. 1329–1384) of England. Wycliffe was a priest and a learned, admired professor of philosophy and theology at Oxford University. He attacked abuses in the Church and denied many long-held beliefs. Of particular importance was his teaching on the Eucharist. Wycliffe held that the bread and wine did not change in the consecration at Mass. This teaching denied the Church's doctrine of the Eucharist.

Wycliffe also denied the authority of the pope, of tradition, and of councils. He said that all Christians were equal in rank and authority under Christ and that all could exercise the functions that had been restricted to bishops and priests.

Wycliffe held that the Bible was the sole rule of faith and that each one was free to read it and interpret it for himself or herself. He wanted to abolish many current religious practices such as veneration of the saints because "Jesus Christ and his apostles used them not." Kings and other secular rulers, Wycliffe said, should take temporal possessions away from churchmen and church institutions. Neither the pope nor the clergy should hold land or property or have a church income. Instead, they should be provided with only the basic necessities of life by the rulers.

Wycliffe's teachings were rejected by most Catholic Christians in England. The greatest response came from the poorer classes and a few diocesan priests.

The Council of Constance (1415) condemned many of Wycliffe's teachings. It was feared that his ideas denied long-held beliefs and practices of the Church and that they would undermine all authority in the Church. History would show that Wycliffe was in many ways a major forerunner of Protestant ideas.

27. In Bohemia, John Huss led a movement in favor of Wycliffe's teachings. Huss was condemned by the Council of Constance and executed. This led to the Hussite Wars of 1415–1434.

During these centuries, as in every era, many good, hard-working people in the Church tried to follow the example of its founder, Christ. Thanks to the work of these dedicated bishops, priests, and lay men and women, the Church educated people, cared for the sick, and—most important—preached the gospel message. These people hoped that the Church would reform and correct the abuses in its management.

Greed for money caused many of the Church's problems. For example, some highly-placed church officials—such as bishops and abbots—sold the church offices under their control to the highest bidder. If a parish needed a pastor, a dishonest bishop might sell the job to the priest who paid him the most money. Sometimes the priest did not even live in his parish and did not do his priestly work for the people. But he still received his salary and the income from parish lands.

Lay people, too, were greedy. Powerful people—lords, rich merchants, kings—forced bishops and priests to obey them. Sometimes these overlords took large sums of money from the Church, or took its treasures. It seemed as though some church leaders were not able to show people how to follow Christian standards in daily life.

In Bohemia, people were very critical of the Church. (Bohemia is the western half of modern Czechoslovakia.) Besides objecting to the greed and scandalous living among some church people, the Bohemians wanted to have their own bishops, not German bishops.

A number of popular preachers in Bohemia preached church reform and the revival of national loyalty. John Huss, one of these preachers, was also a priest and a scholar who taught at the University of Prague.

Huss had read Wycliffe's works, and liked what Wycliffe wrote about going back to the law of Christ and living in accordance with Christ's life. However, some of Wycliffe's other teachings were condemned by the pope as false doctrine. The archbishop of Prague ordered people to bring their copies of Wycliffe's works to his courtyard, where they were burned. But Huss continued to preach and to praise much of Wycliffe's thought, and he asked the people of Prague for support. He even appealed to the pope, and he was ordered to come to Rome to answer charges of heresy, or false belief. Huss refused and was excommunicated by his archbishop.

After several years of disputing and hiding, Huss went to Constance, where the bishops had assembled in council, to defend his ideas. The emperor and Huss's archbishop had promised that he would be safe, but they broke their promises. Huss was tried for heresy, condemned, and burned.

The Bohemian people were furious and fought against the Germanic nations in a series of wars called the Hussite Wars. Gradually, peace and the faith of the Church returned to Bohemia, but John Huss's spirit of nationalism remained.

28. During the Hundred Years War between England and France, Joan of Arc— believing she was guided by heavenly voices— came forth to lead the French army. Joan won a great victory at Orléans, and then persuaded the French prince to be crowned king. Later Joan became a prisoner of the English, was tried by a church court, and burned as a heretic.

In the kingdoms of western Europe great changes were taking place. Some kings were trying to increase their own power and reduce that of their noble vassals by appointing their own government administrators rather than relying on the nobles. Military and administrative costs created a demand for more money and more taxes. This led to fights with the nobility at home and to increased tensions abroad. The Holy Roman Empire was distant and weak. Various states fought fiercely for new territories.

The Hundred Years War between France and England (it actually lasted from 1337 to 1453) was the most striking example of conflicting claims by kings who wanted to unite huge territories under one central government. Joan of Arc, a sixteen-year-old peasant girl from Domrémy, was both the heroine and the victim of this situation. Waged off and on for years, the war was not going well for France. Then Joan, prompted by heavenly voices, set out to help the heir to the throne of France. She led a French army to free the city

of Orléans from siege and won other victories for the French. She persuaded the hesitant Charles to be crowned as King Charles VII of France at Rheims in July 1429. The next year she was captured by Frenchmen who were enemies of the French king. They sold her to the English.

Joan was a mystic, entirely given over to the inspiration and activity of the Lord. As she put it: "All I have done, I have done at the command of God and his angels. . . . It pleased God to work thus, through a simple girl." She put her invincible faith in God's divine action.

Her English captors turned her over to the Inquisition in Rouen. She was tried for heresy and witchcraft and threatened with torture. Alone and frightened, she went back on her claims that she had had divine visions. Later, though, she courageously reaffirmed them. Joan was found guilty of the charges and turned over to the secular court. On May 30, 1431, she was burned at the stake as a heretic.

Today there is little historical doubt about Joan's sincerity and straightforward simplicity, which shines through her testimony. There is also little doubt about the shoddiness of the court proceedings against her.

The French drew new energy from her example and managed to beat back the English. Charles VII, who had done nothing to help Joan during her trial, ordered a retrial for the already-dead young woman. In 1456 her condemnation was annulled, and in 1920 the Church declared her a saint.

29. Bernardine of Siena, who lived in the fifteenth century, preached forcefully to the faithful, asking that they build a truly Christian society. He emphasized that business and commercial methods should agree with Christian principles of justice.

Many of the parish clergy were so poorly educated that they could not properly perform such important duties as preaching, hearing confessions, and helping people apply Christianity to their daily lives. This lack was remedied to some extent by better-educated Dominican and Franciscan friars, who preached repentance, mercy, and civil reconciliation in the streets and public squares. Sometimes they were accompanied by authorized confessors and notaries. The confessors heard people's confessions after the sermons. The notaries drew up official contracts of reconciliation between feuding families, and contracts promising donations to hospitals, orphanages, and other charitable works.

One of the most effective preachers in approaching the common people was Bernardine of Siena. He came from a noble family and had studied classics and law at the University of Siena. He then studied theology and Sacred Scripture. While he was taking care of plague victims, he himself fell ill. After he was cured he entered the Franciscan order. In his early years as a religious, he devoted himself to studying and compiling the works of great theologians and spiritual writers, particularly Franciscan ones.

When Bernardine began to preach he quickly attracted people by his simple explanations, his deep insight, and his forceful devotion to the faith. In the early years of his apostolic work, Bernardine hoped to get rid of the weapons that divided Christians by promoting devotion to the Holy Name of Jesus as the only standard and coat of arms for all Christians. But some churchmen thought this new devotion might be mere superstition, so they instituted church proceedings against Bernardine three times. Each time the Church recognized the truth of his teaching, the rightness of his intention, and the holiness of his life. He was offered the chance to become a bishop, but he refused.

Besides trying to reform the life-style of the people, Bernardine wanted to keep his order faithful to the ideals of Francis of Assisi and to promote theological studies. In 1440 he instituted the study of moral theology in Perugia, and he himself taught there. The following year he organized a center in Siena for future teachers of theology.

Besides promoting devotion to the Holy Name of Jesus, Bernardine had special devotion to the Virgin Mary as the mediatrix between human beings and Jesus, and to Mary's husband Joseph. The basic principles of Christian economics were another matter of concern to him. Bernardine recognized the value of wealth as an instrument for social progress and charitable works. But he urged people to be moderate in pursuing money and other possessions, and he insisted that business and commerce should never violate the basic principles of Christian justice.

30.
At the Council of Florence
in 1439, officials
of the Eastern and Western
Church joined in a decree
reuniting the Church.
But the Byzantine people
did not accept the decree
and the schism continued.

In 1438 Pope Eugene IV convened a church council in Ferrara, Italy, to attempt reunification with the Eastern Church. The Doge (ruler) of Venice invited Eastern church leaders to attend. Since the general sessions led to muddled arguments and debates, small groups or committees were selected to discuss the problems. Dialogue would be easier in these small groups, it was felt.

There was the danger of an epidemic, and there were also financial problems. The pope had to foot the bill for the Eastern delegation, which included the Byzantine emperor, the patriarch of Constantinople, and about seven hundred attendants. So the council was transferred to Florence, where Cosimo de Medici assumed the expenses involved. Discussions were resumed, although they often ended in harsh debates. But there was a strong desire for unity, and no position was irreconcilable. For unity was needed if the Byzantine empire and Constantinople were to be defended against the Ottoman Turks.

Finally, on July 6, 1439, the decree of union between the Eastern and the Western Church was drawn up in both Greek and Latin. It was signed by the pope, the Western bishops, the Byzantine emperor, and the representatives of the Eastern patriarchs (except for Metropolitan Marcus Eugenius of Ephesus). It could not be said that either side had convinced the other by virtue of its reasoning process. The Byzantine representatives, in particular, were not enthusiastic about the decree.

And then there was the hostile attitude of the Eastern clergy and lay people toward Rome and the West. For four centuries they had been opposing the Roman Church and its claims to be the central authority in the Church. Besides, there were still bitter memories of how the Crusaders had looted Constantinople. Now the Byzantines were suddenly supposed to pay homage to the pope and to become friends with families and groups whom they had been at odds with for years. The reaction of the Eastern populace against union with Rome drove the majority of the Eastern signers of the decree to change their minds. The Eastern emperor could never bring himself to promulgate the union, even though urged to by the patriarch.

The attempt to unite the Church, split since 1054, had failed. The split continues to this day.

31. In 1453, Constantinople fell to the Muslim Turks, and the 1000-year-old Byzantine Empire ended. Scholars fled from Constantinople to Italy and other western lands, bringing with them many ancient manuscripts and their knowledge of the Greek language.

For a thousand years the Byzantine Empire had been a rich, powerful center of religion, culture, art, and politics. But now it was falling apart. Court officials and military leaders had quarreled fiercely. Crusaders from the Latin West had weakened the emperor's power.

From the twelfth century on, Turkish tribes and their Islamic religion had become better organized and stronger. In the Balkans, the Serbs had won an uneasy independence from Byzantium. (Their independence was threatened by Venice and ultimately—in 1389—was lost to the Turks.)

These Ottoman Turks, whom we have met before, already possessed Anatolia (Asia Minor). In the fifteenth century they began the conquest of the Balkans. By 1425 the Byzantine Empire had been reduced to Constantinople and the area immediately around it.

The Byzantine emperors begged the Latin West for military and economic help. The popes also appealed to Christian rulers to unite against the Muslim Turks. But Western rulers were too busy fighting each other and trying to increase their own power.

Mohammed II, a great Muslim commander and the real founder of the Ottoman Empire, laid siege to Constantinople, using the largest cannons yet built. After fifty days, on May 29, 1453, Constantinople fell. The Byzantine Empire had come to an end.

When Constantinople fell, scholarly refugees fled to Italy and other Western countries. Their knowledge of Greek, plus the ancient Greek manuscripts they brought with them, contributed to the revival of classical learning that was already under way in the West.

Mohammed II transferred his capital to Constantinople and turned the basilica of Saint Sophia into a mosque or Islamic church. (Much later, it became a museum, as it is today.) Christians were now second-class citizens and had to live in a kind of urban serfdom. The city, which today is called Istanbul, later regained its greatness. For several centuries the military skill and advanced technology of the Turks would threaten the West.

32. Some of the learned monks
who fled from Constantinople
took refuge in Russia,
where an intense monastic
form of spirituality
was lived. At this time
in Russia, the painting
of icons—religious pictures
—was brought to greatness
by Theophanes the Greek
and Andrei Rublev.

The fall of Constantinople shocked all of Christendom but especially the Byzantines. Byzantines had been sure that their thousand-year-old city, built by Constantine, would last forever. But now even its patriarch (the most important bishop in the Eastern churches) was under the rule of Muslim Turks.

This catastrophe, though, led to a new flowering of Orthodox Christianity in Slavic-speaking Russia. From the very beginning of its Christian history, Russia had had close ties to the Byzantine Church. Monks from Byzantium had always visited Russia. Others took refuge there as the Turks advanced and after Constantinople had fallen. They brought with them much of the rich traditions of the Byzantine Empire.

The Russians felt that they had every right to take over the Byzantine heritage. They had not accepted the church union promulgated by the Council of Florence in 1439, and they felt that Constantinople had abandoned the true Orthodox faith in accepting it. In fact, they broke off church relations with Constantinople because of it. And they viewed the fall of the city in 1453 as a punishment from God.

The Russian Church already had a strong tradition of its own. Its monastic life had developed greatly in the thirteenth century. The Mongol overlords who invaded Russia at that time treated the people harshly and taxed them heavily, but they protected the Church and exempted it from taxes. The Church grew wealthy.

In the fourteenth century, Sergius began to reform monastic life and founded the famous Monastery of the Trinity. In the next century, monasteries were built all over Russia. Russian missionaries were active outside of Russia in the fifteenth and sixteenth centuries.

Russian church art was thriving too. In 1425 the monk Andrei Rublev painted an icon of the Holy Trinity that became the model for Russian icons and for representations of the Trinity. It is still known as the icon of icons. Theophanes the Greek painted beautiful frescoes.

Near the end of the fifteenth century an important Christian scholar and humanist named Maximus the Greek came to Russia. Maximus had studied in Greece and Italy. He translated many Greek religious and liturgical works and tried to reform monastic life. Also, he publicly attacked the Russian clergy for what he called their cowardly obedience to civic authority. Maximus wanted a poor Church that would be spiritually independent and speak out against bad rulers.

33. Humanism, which emphasized the creativity and thought of the individual person, had been developing in the West for some time. Now Christian humanists began to study the philosophy and arts of the ancient Greeks and Romans. Old Greek manuscripts and the documents of the early Roman Church were also examined carefully. Lorenzo Valla and Besarion were important people in this movement.

When we talk about humanism in this period of history, we are talking about a renewed interest in, and love for, the languages, literature, and culture of ancient Greece and Rome. There was a minor strain of anti-Christian thought in some humanists, but most of them were devout or convinced Christians who hoped to give new life to Christendom by learning from the great figures of ancient Greece and Rome. For example, humanists now imitated the ancient philosophers by strongly stressing the dignity of nature and of human beings. They also felt that the active civil life of the ancient Greeks and Romans was a fine model of adult, fully developed humanity. Gradually, too, some scholarly humanists began to study the ancient Christian Church as a model for correcting the ills of the Christendom of their own day.

A scholarly humanist and researcher of that time was Lorenzo Valla. He served under Pope Nicholas V. Lorenzo proved that some of the documents used by popes to claim territorial rights in Italy were forgeries. He showed that the so-called Donation of Constantine, in particular, was a forgery that had probably been written in the eighth century. He also examined the New Testament and wondered whether the Apostles' Creed had really been written by the apostles. The methods used by Valla may well be regarded as the start of modern textual criticism.

Another important scholar was Besarion, a Byzantine humanist. After attending the Council of Ferrara-Florence, Besarion remained in Italy and was made a cardinal of the Roman Church. He was a student of Neoplatonic ideas, and he contributed many fine Greek manuscripts to St. Mark's library in Venice.

Some humanists looked for carvings, pieces of sculpture, pillars from old temples that were left from ancient Roman times. In the ruins of old buildings, they found many interesting and important things that they studied to learn about the past.

34. Near the beginning of the fifteenth century, the city of Florence became the home for new trends in literature and art. The Medici family directed much of this cultural activity.

As European society began to change in the fifteenth century, two areas were particularly active. The city of Florence and the region of Flanders were known for their independent cities, their commerce, and their banking operations, as well as for their cultural activities.

The city of Florence was an especially outstanding pioneer in earning wealth and promoting new cultural trends. And when we speak of Florence, we immediately think of the Medici family. Florence had a republican tradition (wherein the people really had a voice in government), but a faction of the rich merchants led by the Albizzi family took control of the city in the early part of the fifteenth century. An unsuccessful war against the commune of Lucca led to the fall of the Albizzi in 1434 and the rise of the Medici family to power.

For almost sixty years the Medici family guided the destiny of Florence. They had come from a rural area, settled in Florence around 1200, and gradually become rich merchants, businessmen, and bankers. Banking was one of the noticeable new activities in western Europe, and it often centered around

the handling of royal and papal finances. The shrewd Medici guided Florence well, were very popular, and did much to eliminate violence. The two outstanding figures in the family were Cosimo de Medici and his grandson known as Lorenzo the Magnificent.

The fame of Florence in this period was due even more to its artistic and cultural life than to its financial activities. Byzantine Greeks got a taste of Florence when Cosimo de Medici served as host for the council there. Some returned later, bringing with them various manuscripts of pagan and Christian classics written in Greek. The libraries of Florence housed these classics and provided great opportunities for scholarly study. Cosimo and Lorenzo Medici did much to subsidize the purchase of manuscripts as well as to encourage great art and architecture. Artists were eager to show them their works. Lorenzo himself was a very good poet, and it was during this period of behind-the-scenes rule that the cultural renaissance of Florence reached its high point. Artists of great talent and even genius could be sure that both their works and their person would be honored in that city.

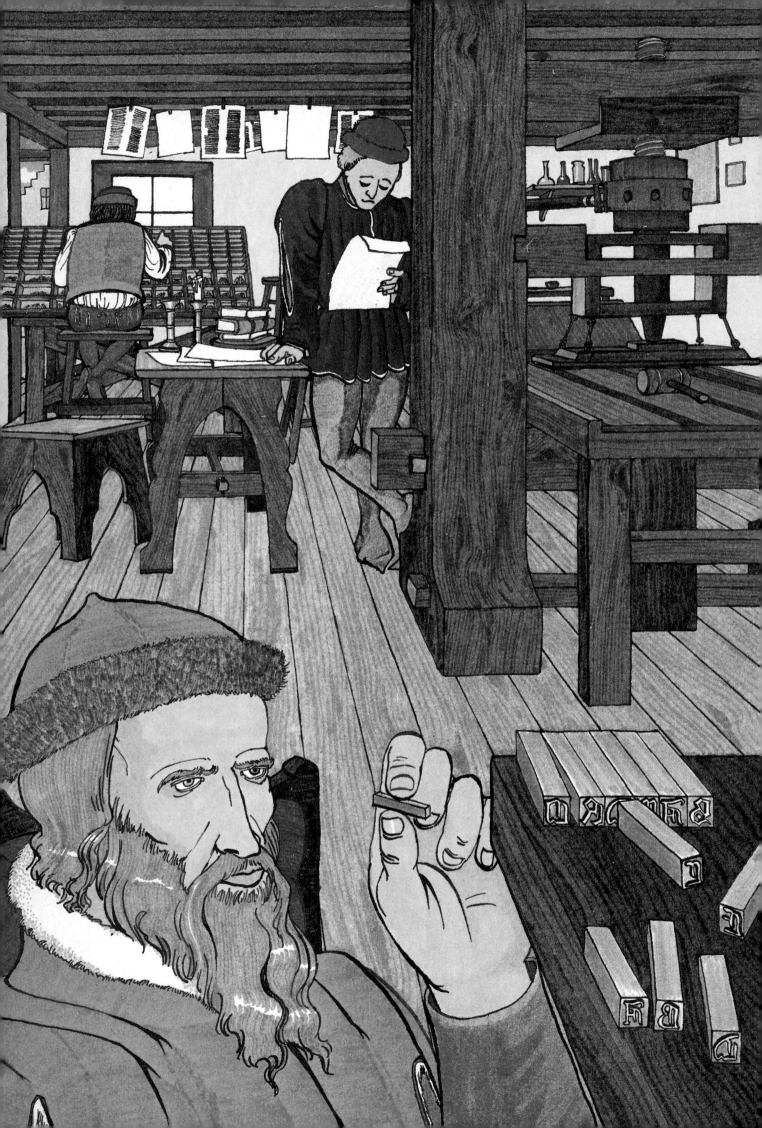

35. Around the year 1450, movable, interchangeable type was invented, making printed books less costly and easier to manufacture than they had been.
More people began to own and read books.
This led to a faster rate in the change of ideas and attitudes and helped spread knowledge that led to new inventions.
But printing and reading had a gradual rather than an immediate influence on people's lives.

The Chinese were using block printing by the end of the sixth century A.D. In block printing, the words and pictures to be printed are carved on a block of wood. Then linen paper is pressed against the inked wooden blocks to get a printed page. It took hundreds of years for this printing process to reach the West, but wood engravings and block-printed books were being made in Europe by the early fifteenth century. This was an expensive and time-consuming way to make books.

The Chinese went on to invent movable type. Around the middle of the fifteenth century a German printer—Johann Gutenberg of Mainz—had the same idea. Gutenberg made individual metal letters instead of wooden blocks, and the letters were set in place by hand. After the page was printed, the letters were sorted out and used again. They could be used many times over. The printing process became much less expensive, and soon many more copies of books were being printed, and fairly rapidly. The new process was soon accepted.

Within fifty years there were printing presses based on movable type in more than a hundred European towns and cities. More than thirteen thousand editions and four million volumes were printed during the fifteenth century.

The impact of the printed book on European life was gradual rather than immediately revolutionary. New and valuable editions of the Bible and ancient classical works were published. So were works by authors of the day. But most of the books printed were the traditional favorites of the Middle Ages, whether they were school texts, sermon books, or fiction works of chivalry and romantic action. The continued increase in new schools and universities during the fifteenth century had created a larger public able to read books. But if booksellers wanted to make a living and a profit, they had to publish the books that people would buy and read. This new way of printing was a valuable instrument for publicizing new ideas and debates, and it would often pay its way by printing the works that people were reading. Throughout the fifteenth and sixteenth centuries, the surviving writings of the Middle Ages were printed and circulated regularly.

Los Altos United Methodist Church Library

36. The arts in western Europe entered a time of high creativity in the 1400s. Humanist Renaissance artists, who put the human person at the center of life and art, produced glorious sculptures, paintings, and buildings. The city of Florence was the center of this humanist, creative activity.

During the fifteenth century, great changes took places in Italian sculpture, painting, and architecture. Florence was the vital center of this humanist creativity, which the Medici supported. The effects gradually spread to many parts of Europe, which also made their own changes.

Renaissance artists combined at least four elements in their works: ancient Greco-Roman elements; a new interest in sciences such as anatomy, geometry, and mathematics; Neoplatonic outlooks; and pervading all, the Christian view of life. Here is what that means.

Like the Greeks and Romans, humanist artists put the human being at the center of life and art (that is why they are called humanists). Greco-Roman sculptors and painters had portrayed the human body realistically. So did Renaissance sculptors and painters, and their new knowledge of anatomy further stimulated this realistic portrayal. Donatello's sculpture of Gattamelata on horseback (shown here) reveals a majestic Roman-like hero, but the anatomical realism of both horse and rider is definitely Renaissance also. We see the same realism in Florentine paintings and church sculpture, and Flemish paintings are known for their realistic detail throughout.

Florentine architects planned splendid buildings, among them the beautiful cathedral of St. Mary of the Flowers, whose dome is shown here. Some of their buildings imitated the symmetry of the human body (notice the paired features of the windows in our illustration) and showed the age's interest in geometry and mathematics. Painters, too, balanced their paintings precisely. For instance, a composition might have three important points that would form a triangle. Or one group of people would formally balance another, as in the Mystical Lamb by the Flemish artist Van Eyck.

Humanist Renaissance artists, with their new interest in science, also discovered perspective. They noticed, for instance, that a person seems to grow smaller as he or she walks farther away. So they learned to paint objects smaller to make them look far away.

Renaissance artists also combined Neoplatonism (the "new" Platonism) in their works. Neoplatonism said that the soul could ascend toward union with God by contemplating beauty. This spiritual, mystical, Neoplatonic quality of Renaissance art shows everywhere.

Renaissance painting, sculpture, and architecture was of course pervasively Christian: The favorite subjects were still biblical scenes, the Madonna, and the saints.

Humanism

37.

To help us understand
the daily life of people
during the Renaissance,
we will read the story
of a merchant family
in Florence around 1450.
In our story, Anselm and
Angela combine
a busy life in the city
with a quiet life
on their rural estate.
They have three children—
twin sons and a daughter.

Anselm, the husband in our imaginary family in Florence, was a successful textile merchant. He had added to his family's wealth by importing spices and luxury goods from the East and selling them in the West at a profit.

Anselm seemed to be a less-wealthy copy of Cosimo de Medici, the wealthy merchant and banker who ran the government of Florence from behind the scenes. Florence was organized as a republic, but Cosimo de Medici was the real ruling power. Most Florentines were glad to have him in charge because of his strong leadership, his ability to organize things, and his encouragement of art and literature. Cosimo was a sincere Christian, and now and then he left the busy city to spend time in prayer and contemplation in a monastery.

Unlike Cosimo, Anselm had little to do with the government of the city-state of Florence. But Anselm, too, liked to withdraw from the bustle of business to live in the quiet of the country. He and his wife Angela had a country estate near Florence. This was a large home surrounded by farmlands and vineyards tilled by workers and tenants.

Anselm's wife Angela was in charge of the estate and farms. Energetic and intelligent, she made the estate a prosperous business as well as a charming home for her family.

Anselm's textile and farm workers and tenants felt that he treated them justly. From time to time Anselm gave money to the Church, and he financed the building of a parish church near his country estate. Anselm also gave money to confraternities to help the members carry out their works of charity.

The couple had three children: twin boys named John and Guido, and a daughter named Matilda. The children spent much of their time in the country, but lived for part of each year in Florence. There the boys liked to visit their father's shop and examine the beautiful things stored there.

38. John, one of the sons in our imaginary family, went on a long trip before he began to work in his father's business. He visited China, India, and Flanders, combining business activities with travel. After four years he returned home, ready to take over the family business.

Angela and Anselm hired scholars to come to their home to teach their children. Even Matilda was educated. Up until this time, women usually did not learn to read and write, but now upper-class families were educating their daughters as well as their sons.

John was especially interested in traveling. At their country home he would often take long rides on horseback, imagining himself traveling in faraway lands. In the city of Florence he would try to be near when his father did business with men from other lands who visited the shop.

Guido was interested in study of all kinds, but especially in the study of foreign languages and in history.

Matilda was deeply interested in art and all works of beauty, both those made by people and those made by nature.

When the twin sons were about seventeen, John asked his father to allow him to travel for several years before he settled down into the family business. The knowledge he would

gain about other countries would be helpful to him when he became a textile merchant and importer, he pointed out. And of course John had always wanted to travel.

Anselm agreed, and John began his travels by going on a long business trip with a family friend. They went east to India and China, and then northwest to Antwerp in Flanders. Antwerp was growing in commercial and financial importance. More and more merchants, such as Anselm, brought their luxury cargoes to Antwerp for resale. The diamond industry was becoming important there.

John traveled from place to place for four years, coming home to Florence for a visit only once during this time. Good reports about John came back to his father. John seemed to be a fine business man, and he made many useful business contacts.

When John returned for good, his family welcomed him happily. Guido and Matilda listened for hours to the stories of his travels, and Anselm and Angela were eager to know about his business activities. And Anselm, Angelo, Guido, and Matilda had much to tell John also.

39. In our story about a Florentine family, Guido joins a group of philosophers and humanists, and John takes over the family business. Both John and Matilda are married. Some time later, Anselm dies peacefully.

When John returned from his travels, he learned that his sister Matilda was engaged to be married to a young artist. They looked forward to a happy life together, sharing their interest in art and beauty.

John's twin brother, Guido, wanted to become a serious scholar. He hoped that John would become a merchant and work beside their father, Anselm. Then he, Guido, would be free to study. John was agreeable to this plan.

Anselm wanted to retire soon, because he knew that his health was poor. He planned how to divide his property among his family members, and the textile business was turned over to John.

To everyone's surprise, John—after all his travels—fell in love with a young woman named Beatrice who lived on an estate near his own home. So that spring, Anselm's family celebrated two weddings.

Within the following year, the family was deeply saddened by Anselm's death. He was buried in the graveyard of the parish church he had built in the country.

With John running the business, Guido was free to study. He was especially interested in the study of Greek, and traveled to Greece to explore some of the famous cities and landmarks there.

Guido soon became part of a group of humanists and philosophers in Florence. Humanists studied, among other things, history, poetry, and moral philosophy. They especially revered the ancient writers of Greece and Rome and felt that some ideas expressed by these ancient writers were helpful to modern Christians. Humanists also wanted to know many languages, so that they could read the ancient books and share in the knowledge of other lands. And humanists looked for and studied such things as manuscripts, carvings, coins, and medals that still remained in their own country from ancient times. People in Italy now realized that many old manuscripts were mouldering forgotten on the shelves of monastery libraries or in tumbled-down buildings. Humanists wanted to find these old writings before they were lost forever.

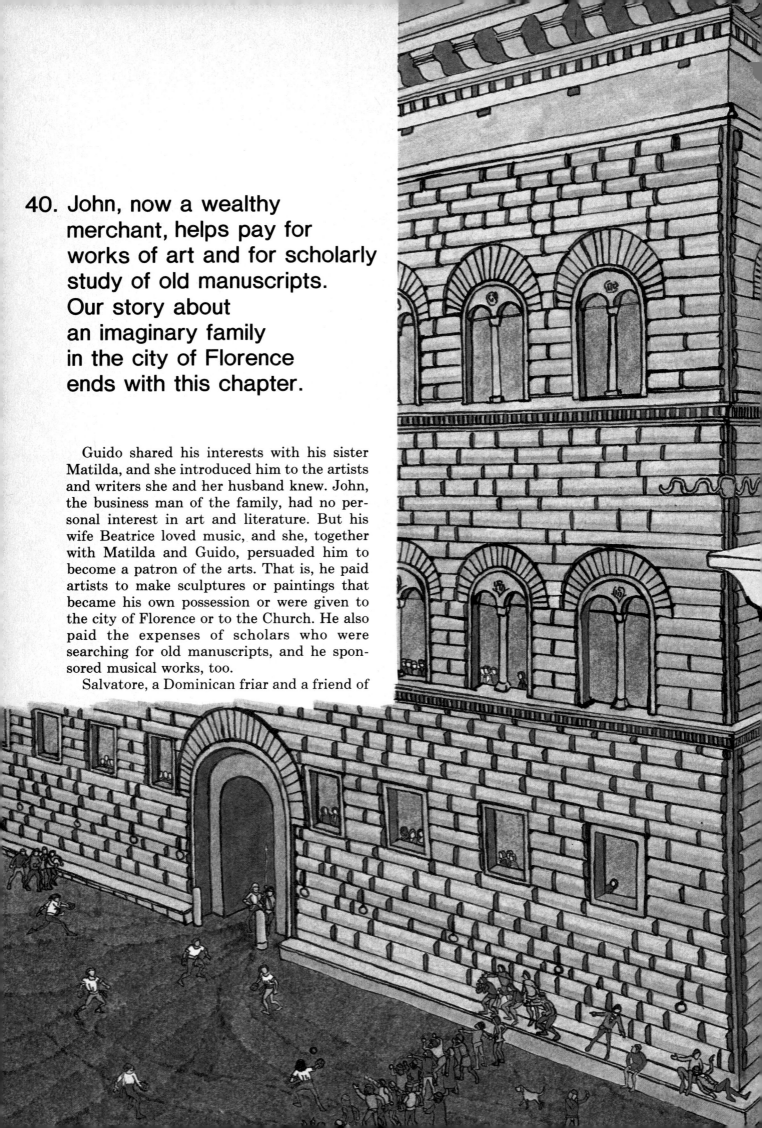

40. John, now a wealthy
merchant, helps pay for
works of art and for scholarly
study of old manuscripts.
Our story about
an imaginary family
in the city of Florence
ends with this chapter.

Guido shared his interests with his sister
Matilda, and she introduced him to the artists
and writers she and her husband knew. John,
the business man of the family, had no personal interest in art and literature. But his
wife Beatrice loved music, and she, together
with Matilda and Guido, persuaded him to
become a patron of the arts. That is, he paid
artists to make sculptures or paintings that
became his own possession or were given to
the city of Florence or to the Church. He also
paid the expenses of scholars who were
searching for old manuscripts, and he sponsored musical works, too.

Salvatore, a Dominican friar and a friend of

Guido, helped persuade John to patronize art and research. Friar Salvatore explained that the arts are one way people are led to contemplate and enjoy the whole of God's creation.

One evening Matilda invited her brothers, John's wife Beatrice, and Friar Salvatore to her home for a supper party. Afterward they talked freely about their feelings regarding the state of the Church.

Friar Salvatore expressed great discouragement about the state of Christian nations. The pope and emperor seemed to hold empty, meaningless titles. Every region or city-state had its own prince or ruler. It was impossible to unite Christians against the Muslims, or even to get Christian kings to make peace with each other.

Guido and Matilda spoke up at that and said that they thought some of the Church's high officials were to blame for many of the problems. Many church leaders seemed more concerned with money, getting favors for their family, and living in a princely way than they were in helping people be Christian. After all,

Cosimo de Medici had managed to have a fourteen-year-old relative be made a cardinal. How could a boy of fourteen fulfill the responsibilities of a cardinal?

Friar Salvatore nodded and said that he knew their complaints were justified. Then, to the surprise of the others, John began to express a more cheerful view. From his experiences on his travels, he felt that Europe was changing for the better. Scholars and merchants were carrying knowledge from one country to another. Individual Muslims seemed like ordinary people when you met them personally, and not like terrifying raiders. There would always be thieves and selfish people in the world, he said, but many others seemed to be trying to live as sincere believers in God. Perhaps, said John, the new pope—Pius II—would lead Europe to more peaceful, prosperous times.

On this optimistic note, the group turned their talk to a happier topic—art and literature and the most recent discoveries of treasures of the past.

41. Nicholas of Cusa, a serious thinker and a dedicated churchman, worked for church reform in the fifteenth century.

Nicholas of Cusa was one of the most interesting figures of the fifteenth century. Born in the Germanic regions, he became a humanist thinker with a deep interest in a wide variety of topics, including philosophy, nature, and the study of the universe. He was a mystical thinker who stressed the limitations of human knowledge. He was a convinced Christian, who gave up a career as a lawyer to become a priest. And he was an active reforming clergyman who spoke out against abuses in the Church.

One abuse that Cusa mentioned was using indulgences as a means of gaining income for the Church. (An indulgence granted by the Catholic Church remits or takes away the temporal punishment due for sin. The person gaining the indulgence does certain acts required by the Church—for example, doing charitable deeds. Going to Confession and receiving the Eucharist are usually part of the conditions for gaining indulgences. Also, certain prayers are to be said, and sometimes a pilgrimage has to be made.) At the time

Nicholas lived, one of the conditions for receiving an indulgence was often an offering of money or goods for the Church or the poor. Unfortunately, the gift of money sometimes seemed to be the most important part of gaining indulgences. Some people thought that they could buy their way into heaven for themselves and their families by giving rich offerings for indulgences. And some priests and bishops, to get more money for themselves, would ask for the money without emphasizing the spiritual things that were more

important than the money offering. This abuse would later cause great trouble in the Church, and around 1450 Nicholas spoke out against it.

Nicholas also worked with Pope Pius II in reforming the clergy of Rome. He also wrote a comprehensive plan for the reform of the Church and the Empire. Sad to say, the plan for reform was not followed by the whole Church.

Nicholas was a cardinal and had heavy duties in the service of the pope, and he was also the bishop of a diocese. Yet he continued to ponder theological questions. In him, the mystical and deeply religious concerns of the *Devotio Moderna* (New Devotion) seemed to combine with the newer interests of the Italian Renaissance. He stressed the limitations of human beings in trying to come to a knowledge of God. Nicholas believed that we discover God only through our intuition, that is, through insight or understanding that comes without a reasoning process.

42. The new enthusiasm
for the ancient classical
world and its written
and artistic works
led to the establishment
of academies
where scholars, artists,
and lovers of the ancient
languages and literature
met to study and work
together. One of the
most famous academies
was in Florence.

The new enthusiasm for the writings of antiquity, and especially for the ideals of human dignity and beauty they expressed, led to the establishment of Academies. Imitating those in ancient Greece, the new Academies enlisted educators, artists, scholars, politicians, and religious figures for group discussion in such fields as philosophy, religion, art, textual criticism, and translation. Some academies collected examples of classical Greek and Roman art.

The first and most famous of these Academies was the Platonic Academy of Florence. It was founded shortly after the middle of the fifteenth century with the support and encouragement of Cosimo de Medici. Its members studied and commented on the work of Plato and later followers of his tradition (Neoplatonists). The guiding spirit of this Academy was Marsilio Ficino (1433–1499), who translated many of Plato's and Plotinus's works from Greek into Latin.

The Academy was not interested in abstract philosophy but taught a whole way of speaking, thinking, and living. Platonic phi-

losophers, both pagan and Christian ones, stressed the soul, spiritual beauty, mystical experience, inward goodness, and the harmony seen in nature. Indeed, Ficino wrote an original work in which he tried to combine Christian theology with such Platonic ideas.

Members of the Academy were not always deep scholars, but they were interested in the real values found in ancient Greek and Roman culture, and they tried to combine them with Christian values and the whole Christian way of life.

43. John Pico della Mirandola attempted to unite the faith of the Middle Ages with the new humanistic enthusiasm for human achievements. He was a man of genius, and put together his own system of knowledge.

Another truly interesting figure of the fifteenth century was John Pico della Mirandola. He was a member of the Platonic Academy in Florence, and he was greatly admired by Marsilio Ficino, a leader at the Academy, who was about thirty years older than he was.

But John Pico, Count of Mirandola, was not interested in just one current of thought; nor could he remain the disciple of just one teacher. He was a man of genius who tried to cover many fields of knowledge in his brief lifetime of thirty-one years. He was in touch with many rich and deep currents of thought in his day, and he tried to show that those currents could be fused with Christian ideas to form a new synthesis.

Pico's short life was full and active. He studied and wrote at a feverish pace, driven

on by an unquenchable thirst for knowledge. Languages, literature, philosophy, and other subjects absorbed him. At an early age he envisioned a great project which he felt his age needed. After eight years of intense study he put together his own system of knowledge, his own organization of all the various subjects. He formulated nine hundred theses (or statements of ideas) and offered to debate them. Theologians and philosophers were invited to Rome. But many were opposed to his project, and there were suspicions that some of his theses did not conform to Christian doctrine. The pope suspended the proposed debate, and some of the theses were later considered heretical. Another argument with the Church led to a brief imprisonment in France. Then Pico returned to Florence and became a close friend of Girolamo Savonarola.

One of Pico's famous works was his *Oration on the Dignity of the Human Being.* Human grandeur, said Pico, lay in the fact that God had put into human beings the seeds for any and every sort of life. Human beings could choose to degrade themselves to the level of lower beasts, or they could choose to be reborn to a higher life and to become more like God himself. To the human being it is granted "to have whatever it chooses, to be whatever it wills."

At his death Christian Europe mourned and praised him. Girolamo Savonarola, whom we will meet in the next chapter, expressed the sentiments of many in his famous funeral eulogy: "Perhaps no mortal was touched with greater genius. . . . This man must be considered one of the miracles of God and of nature by virtue of his lofty spirit and teaching."

44. Girolamo Savonarola,
a moral reformer, became
for a time the ruler
of Florence. His fanatic
zeal brought him into
conflict with the Church
and with Florentines.
He was imprisoned, tried,
condemned, and executed.

In 1482, Girolamo Savonarola, a Dominican friar in Florence, preached forcefully against the sinful lives of many lay people and priests. Savonarola was not a native Florentine but had come to that city from Bologna. He worked for moral reform, and at first was supported by the powerful Medici family.

But in furthering reform, Savonarola was an extremist and a fanatic. He began to take part in violent political affairs, claiming that he was justified by visions from God.

When King Charles VIII of France invaded Italy in 1494, Savonarola welcomed him, claiming that God had sent Charles to punish the Church and its sinful people. Charles overthrew the Medici family, the ruling power in Florence. For the next four years, Savonarola was the real ruler of Florence.

Savonarola was a loyal Christian and a dedicated religious person. For a time, he combined these qualities with his power as ruler. Under Savonarola's leadership, people's behavior improved—at least outwardly.

Florentines were fond of luxuries and owned beautiful works of art. Savonarola looked on some of these things as throwbacks to pagan times, and he demanded that they be burned. Some people, convinced by his powerful preaching, brought their own things to the city square and threw them into the fire. Others gave them up unwillingly to bands of Savonarola's followers.

Savonarola also tried forcibly to change the state of affairs in the Church. At that time, the pope—Alexander VI—was known to be a very wicked man. Savonarola demanded that a council be called to depose the pope.

Savonarola lost the support of many Florentines, and he was taken prisoner by a mob and put on trial. He was tortured until he confessed that he had done wrong. When the torture stopped, he took back his confession. He was condemned to death and was hanged.

Girolamo Savonarola was one of the last of the zealous reformers of the Middle Ages. He was a very complicated person in a very complicated situation, and his story is tragic. Unfortunately, in this short chapter, only an outline of his life and motives can be given.

45. Friar Bernardine of Feltre was deeply concerned about the poor who could not afford to borrow money because of the high interest rates. He founded an institution to provide money for the needy at reasonable charges.

Martin Tomitano was born in Feltre, Italy, in 1439. He entered the Franciscan Order and took the name Bernardine in honor of Bernardine of Siena. Like the earlier Bernardine, he was an active preacher.

From his early youth, the intelligent young man loved reading and made rapid strides in humanistic studies. At the age of eleven he was reading and speaking Latin with ease. As a student of law at the University of Padua he was admired for his keen mind and his serious life-style. Then he entered the Franciscan Order, studied theology in Venice, and was ordained a priest. His first assignment was to teach grammar. Next, his superiors commissioned him as a preacher. He was a preacher until his death, traveling all of central and southern Italy and often meeting fierce opposition.

Bernardine's activity astounded many of his contemporaries. They could not see how such a frail-looking creature could do such strenuous work. He was sickly and afflicted with tuberculosis. But his preaching drew large crowds, and big cities competed to hear him. In his sermons he encouraged devotion to Mary, strongly criticized evil habits, and urged people to love their neighbors—particularly the poor and defenseless.

Another major theme in his preaching was unjust practices and their consequences. Human beings could fully express themselves only through their labor, he said. It was necessary to help people do this, not to plunge them into wretched poverty through usury (excessive interest rates on loans). So Bernardine of Feltre encouraged the establishment of lending institutions or banks where artisans and other workmen could obtain loans at reasonable rates of interest. (At the time it was not unusual for interest rates to range as high as 60% or even 80%.) His lending institutions were known as *Monti di Pietà* (Mountains of Pity), and the term remains in Italian today as another name for pawnshop. These institutions were founded in such places as Mantua (1484), Padua (1491), Crema and Pavia (1493). Bernardine's institutions did not cause usury to disappear, but they certainly helped to reduce the harsh plight of some people.

Bernardine met much opposition from his fellow friars on one point. Unlike them, he maintained that it was legal and right to ask for a fair and reasonable interest-payment on a loan of money. This was necessary, he said, for the continued functioning of banking organizations.

Bernardine's social work never drew him away from his work as a preacher. He stopped preaching only a few days before his death in 1494, when his illness prevented him from going on.

46.
Catherine Fieschi
of Genoa and her husband
led a group of Christians
who served the poor
by working in their homes,
caring for the sick,
and helping needy people
in any way possible.

In 1447 Catherine Fieschi was born into a noble family in Genoa, Italy. She was given a religious and humanistic education. At the age of thirteen she wanted to become a nun in the same monastery where her sister was. But she was not yet old enough, and her family had other plans. At the age of sixteen she was pushed into marrying a young nobleman. The underlying aim was to make peace with the nobleman's powerful family, with whom the Fieschi had had quarrels.

The early years of the marriage were not happy ones for Catherine. Her husband lived lavishly and indulged in all sorts of entertainment, such as excessive gambling and drinking. Catherine herself took part in the high life of the upper class, but this did not bring her contentment. She never lost her high ideals, and she began to have some influence on her husband.

After ten years of marriage, she managed to turn him away from his old habits of immoral living. The two young people moved from their luxurious home to a simple house near a hospital. Then they set to work serving the sick. They began to receive Communion every day, a practice that was not common at that time. Catherine fasted a great deal, but always remained active and lively. Her charitable work was intense and unceasing. She was named rector of the hospital, and so she took on all the tasks of administration and organization without giving up her care for the sick.

She visited the poor in their homes and performed the most lowly tasks for them.

Thanks to the example of such people as Catherine, charitable activity flourished in Genoa, in other Italian cities, and in other areas of western Europe.

47. Desiderius Erasmus dedicated his life to rediscovering the pure and authentic sources of Christian life in the Bible and in the teachings of the Fathers. In his written works, he shared his thought with other Christians.

Desiderius Erasmus was born in Rotterdam in 1446. He was the illegitimate son of a priest. Educated by members of the Brethren of the Common Life, he then entered an Augustinian monastery in order to further his scholarly studies. He went to England, made friends with Thomas More and John Colet, and experienced a religious conversion. The Bible, the Fathers of the Church, and using his language skills for religious purposes would occupy him throughout his life. Erasmus brought out a new Greek edition of the New Testament and editions of the works of St. Jerome and other Fathers of the Church.

The aim of Erasmus was to present people with the "philosophy of Christ." By that he meant the basic teaching and outlook of Jesus. As he put it: "I would like the simple and pure Christ to be deeply impressed on the minds of human beings." To do that, he said, Christians should learn the Bible and the early Church Fathers. In Erasmus we find the hopeful optimism and the love for learning and eloquence of the Italian humanist combined with the deeply religious concerns of the northern Christian.

But Erasmus also had a sharp eye and a sharp tongue, and the sad state of church organization and leadership did not escape his biting pen. In 1502 he noted that a layman considered it an insult to be mistaken for a priest or a monk. Erasmus himself was a priest, so his remark cannot be regarded as a layman's bias. He was a devoted Christian; he hoped to ridicule churchmen, religious, and laity back to good sense. In his famous and popular *Praise of Folly* he wittily and sarcastically criticized theologians, monks, and foolish people who equated religion solely with pilgrimages, relics, and the superficial trappings of devotion. As Erasmus put it: "We kiss the shoes of the saints and their dirty handkerchiefs, and we leave their books, which are their most holy and efficacious relics, neglected."

For Erasmus the revival of humanistic studies was intended to be one phase of the revival of Christianity on all levels. Good scholarship and sound religious sense would lead people to God. Once people came to know the "philosophy of Christ," sound piety and works of charity would flower everywhere.

In early 1517 Erasmus wrote several letters which expressed his optimism and his bright hopes for the future. He saw a golden age coming. Christian princes were learning the arts of peace. The future was bright with promise for learning and piety: "At the present moment I could almost wish to be young again." But events would take a very unexpected turn for Erasmus and western Europe when the Reformation with all its changes occurred.

48. Around the year 1500,
many humanists combined
their serious study
with efforts to bring
about church reform.
Work by sincere,
dedicated churchmen
in Spain, Germany, and
France furthered
the cause of reform.

By the closing years of the fifteenth century, people's passionate interest in ancient languages, classical (Greco-Roman) culture, and the sources of Christian thought had spread widely. The same people often sincerely desired to promote Church reform and revive church life, as we have already seen in the case of Erasmus, Pico della Mirandola, and Nicholas of Cusa. This deeply religious humanism was flourishing around the turn of the sixteenth century, as a few examples will show.

In Spain one churchman truly stood out among his contemporaries: Cardinal Francisco Ximénez de Cisneros. He did much to reform church life in Spain. He fought against such church abuses as selling indulgences and absenteeism (holding a church office and receiving the salary but not being present to perform one's duties). In 1509 he also founded the University of Alcalá de Henares, which soon became one of the best universities in Europe. Students and teachers came from many places to study the ancient sources and give new life to theological studies. The cardinal also sponsored the publication of the Polyglot Bible, a complete edition of the Bible in Hebrew, Syriac, Greek, and Latin. Such a Bible was valuable because it allowed scholars to compare the texts of ancient manuscripts to see if the translations were accurate.

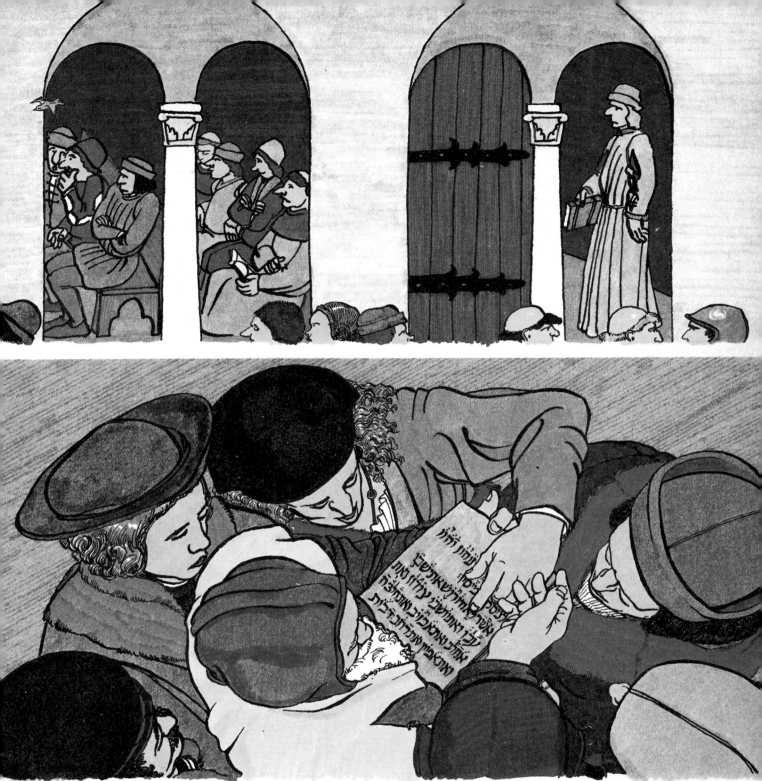

In France a major religious humanist was Jacques Lefèvre d'Étaples. He was renowned as a teacher. He turned from an early interest in Aristotle and his works to religious reform and religious books. He was fascinated by the mystical treatises of such figures as Raymond Lull, but he was also interested in grammar and mathematics. Many of his students were churchmen who wished to see church reform.

In Germany humanism developed around the great centers of the printing industry and around the many new schools that had arisen in the fifteenth century. One outstanding scholar and teacher was Johannes Reuchlin, who developed an interest in the Hebrew language. In 1506 he published the first Hebrew grammar written by a Christian. In Stuttgart he taught a whole generation of students how to read Hebrew, the language of the Old Testament. He fought successfully against bigots who opposed the teaching of Hebrew and who advocated the destruction of all Hebrew books. In fact, he urged that two chairs of Hebrew study be set up in every university in Germany.

49. Eastern Europe was also affected by the spread of humanism. Young students studied in Italy or learned about new trends while living at western courts. They carried the new knowledge home with them.

The kingdoms of Poland-Lithuania, Bohemia, and Hungary had long been a part of Christian Europe. These areas were less influenced by the new humanism than Western Europe was, but contacts with Italy ensured some spread of the new interest. Rulers, noblemen, court attendants, bishops, and other churchmen could not help but be fascinated. Young students came to study in Italy and carried a taste for the new knowledge back home with them, along with examples of Renaissance art.

In Hungary, King Matthias Corvinus welcomed artists and men of letters to his court. His councillor, Archbishop Janos Vitéz, encouraged young noblemen to go to Italy to study. The archbishop and the king both favored the establishment of printing presses. The king also started a distinguished library which survives to this day. This trend was reinforced when Beatrice of Aragon became the king's second wife.

Students, poets, and translators of the Bible were influenced by visits to Italy. Undoubtedly the general atmosphere of humanism helped to inspire the project for universal peace drawn up by King George Podiebrad of Bohemia. His project sought to unite all the European states under one set of laws and to promote joint action against the Turks.

Poland learned something of the new trends from students who had returned from such Italian cities as Bologna, Ferrara, and Padua. Churchmen, such as the Cardinal of Krakow and the Archbishop of Leopoli, were among the first Polish humanists. The middle and lower nobility were also interested. An Italian humanist, Philip Buonaccorsi, spread the influence of Italian humanism at the court of the Polish king. The German humanist, Conrad Celtis, founded a literary society in Krakow. The work of foreign and native humanists helped to spread an interest in Platonism and led to the development of Jagiello University.

**50. The papacy was undergoing
a crisis in leadership
during the latter half
of the fifteenth century.
The popes were humanists
and they encouraged
the arts and literature.
The popes were also rulers.
But they were unable
to enforce church reform,
even though Christians
everywhere wished for it.**

The papacy, too, accepted the movement known as humanism. From the time of Nicholas V's reign (1447–1455), the popes were patrons of scholarship, literature, and the arts. One pope, Pius II (reigned 1458–1464), was himself a true humanist and an accomplished writer. This tradition of humanistic patronage was continued by such later popes as Julius II (reigned 1503–1513) and Leo X (reigned 1513–1521).

Politics and financial concerns also assumed great importance. Since the popes were trying to extend and strengthen their territorial rule in parts of Italy, they needed to make allies and to ensure the neutrality of outside rulers. So they had to make compromises. In some cases this meant giving secular rulers a significant say in running the Church in their country. The most notable example of this was Spain, where the ruler took over control of the Church to a very great extent. The Spanish Inquisition, with all its cruelties and injustice, was, in effect, a tool by which the secular state safeguarded national security and controlled opposition.

Running the Papal States (the territories controlled by the pope) and Rome required a great deal of money. Revenue and bank loans were needed, and it was all too easy to take in money by granting new indulgences, selling

church offices and lands, and making profitable arrangements with kings and princes. Even when the popes were decent men, fear of bankruptcy could involve them in worldly matters and in compromises that did nothing to uphold their role as spiritual leaders. And some of the popes in the fifteenth century were more like scoundrels or political operators, out to benefit themselves, their children, and their relatives in general. Niccolo Machiavelli, who is famous for encouraging rulers to engage in shady dealings, complained that the Church and its leaders set a terrible example for the people.

As we have seen repeatedly, many Europeans were devoutly Christian and yearned for personal holiness and church reform. But somehow the Renaissance papacy never managed to take the lead in uniting these yearnings. A crisis of spiritual leadership faced the Church of Western Christendom, and the most serious consequences would break out before the papacy effectively faced the problem.

51. Spiritual leadership
was poor but most people
of Europe were sincere
Christians. They now had
more printed works,
such as books of prayers
and religious meditations.
Biblical plays, sermons
by traveling preachers,
and large tablets
in churches with the words
of prayers carved on them
were some ways in which
religious education
was brought to the people.

The papacy, dioceses, and parishes were providing little spiritual leadership and were neglecting their people. The people in turn mistrusted clergymen and church dealings generally. But despite all this, European Christians were for the most part loyal to the Church and actively devout. Devotion to the Blessed Virgin and the saints was flourishing. The Rosary, the Angelus, and the Stations of the Cross were popular practices. Many churches were being built, and many religious institutions and groups were being founded.

Unfortunately, though, devotion to the Blessed Virgin and the saints was so popular that sometimes it seemed more important than devotion to Jesus Christ. Moreover, the supreme act of worship, the Mass, posed problems even though the ceremonies might be beautiful and impressive. Most worshipers did not understand Latin, the language of the Mass. There was almost no preaching at Mass except on special occasions. The priest was the only really active person there, it seemed; the lay congregation merely looked on. Many worshipers, too, mistakenly thought that the most important moment at Mass was the elevation of the host after the Consecration. People ran from church to church to be present for that moment and see the consecrated host. That was what "attending Mass" meant to many people.

The religious education of the people came through the work of some specially trained preachers, through sacred plays, and through sacred art seen in stained-glass windows, statues, and paintings. Wise spiritual leaders tried to use other "visual aids." For example, while Nicholas of Cusa was in Germany he had wooden tablets installed in his churches. On them were the texts of the Our Father, the Hail Mary, the Apostles' Creed, and the Ten Commandments. In that way those who could read could learn the elementary prayers and church teachings.

The printing press certainly helped those who could read and encouraged others to learn to read. Only a few could read, but more and more were learning all the time. Thomas More, the scholarly English statesman, estimated that three out of five people in England could read in his time (1478–1535). His estimate may have been a bit high, though. In any case, between 1408 and 1530, more than half the books printed in England were religious books, mostly books of devotion. The same hunger for religious books, especially for small prayer books, works of devotion, and books of sermons, was evident all over western Europe. Religion and piety were clearly important to people.

The Renaissance

52. Beginning with the 1300s, a rebirth of art and learning took place in Italy, and it began to spread through Europe by the end of the 1400s. This rebirth is now called the Renaissance. Michelangelo, Raphael, and Leonardo da Vinci are famous Italian artists who expressed the ideals of this time.

In this book, "Renaissance" refers to the period when Europeans rediscovered the languages, arts, ideals, and institutions of the ancient world. And by "the ancient world" here we mean the Greco-Roman world as it existed before the barbarian invasions that began about 400 A.D. Some people who use the term "Renaissance" think only about the rediscovery of non-Christian culture. But actually there was also a renaissance or rebirth of interest in the early Christian Church. The Renaissance began in Italy in the early 1300s and spread to other western countries.

Renaissance art differed from earlier medieval art and used many classical pagan elements. But in content it was mainly Christian art, not pagan Greek or Roman art. For instance, like pagan art it stressed the human body and human ideals. But with Christian vision it saw the human being as part of God's design. And even when it used pagan charac-

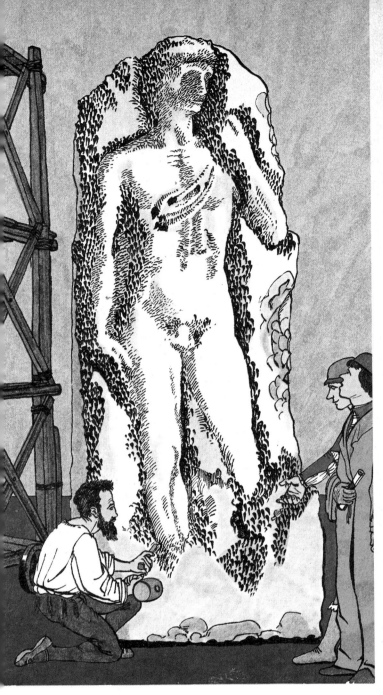

ters, they often symbolized some Christian person or truth.

Three great Italian Renaissance artists were Raphael, Leonardo da Vinci, and Michelangelo.

The paintings of Raphael were filled with movement and color, with beauty and grace. His earlier works were more classical (Greco-Roman) in style, but in his later works he shifted towards a more mystical style which offered a vision of deep religious devotion. His Sistine Madonna, done in 1513, was perhaps the finest example of this later style.

Leonardo da Vinci was an artist, architect, engineer, astronomer, philosopher, poet, and art theorist. He strongly believed that art must be grounded on sound theory, that it must represent things as they are in nature and also depict beauty. A true portrayal of human bodies, emotions, and events required study and constant practice. When done

properly, he said, a painting might capture the beauty and harmony of God's order. His Last Supper, finished in 1498, showed how a masterpiece could combine unity with high drama.

Michelangelo always remained closely associated with Florence and the Medici family. It was there that he sculpted his marvelous, gigantic statue of David. Popes of the Medici family commissioned him to work in Rome as well, where between 1508 and 1512 he executed his stunning frescoes on the ceiling of the Sistine Chapel. In them, too, one can see a shift from his earlier classical style to a more dynamic and mystical style. Michelangelo depicted salvation history in magnificent splendor, and his vision of God the Father seemed to capture the mystery of primeval creation and divine power.

53. The Renaissance spread to northern Europe, and important developments took place in Flanders and Germany. Holbein, Grünewald, and Dürer were famous artists of this period. Religious scenes were the major subject for artistic works during the Renaissance.

In the low countries of the north, the Flemish tradition in art was important. The technique of painting in oil came from there. Flemish art works showed the artists' interest in inner devotion and spiritual contemplation. But at the same time the artists strove to depict family life and civil life with great individuality and realistic detail.

Realism and works in miniature fascinated the people of Flanders. But even in larger art works for their churches, chapels, and homes their attention to detail and color was evident.

The great outpouring of paintings in Flanders during this period was encouraged by the urban middle classes. They wanted to gain prestige and at the same time to express real Christian devotion.

Renaissance art flourished in Germany also. Artists such as Hans Holbein (1465–c.1524) and Matthias Grünewald (c.1475–1528) were important. But somehow Albrecht Dürer (1471–1528) seemed to embody the whole interaction between Italy and northern Europe. In his works the traditions of Gothic art and the influence of painters in northern Europe were combined with firsthand knowledge of Italy and its new directions in art. Again in Dürer we see that Renaissance art was predominantly religious, Christian art. In his writings on art Dürer said that religious art should take first place over any other kind.

Venice was a great city-state, indeed a city-empire. It grew wealthy as the great trading link between the East and the West, and between northern Europe and the Mediterranean. In fact, its interest in wealth seems to

explain why it would not become a flourishing art center until late in the sixteenth century. By that time, the Renaissance had long since swept over much of Italy and other parts of Europe.

But Venice eventually would become a great center for art. Its architecture combined elements of Renaissance harmony with later refinements of the Gothic style and ornamental motifs from the Near East.

The aristocratic merchants of Venice eventually wanted to decorate their fine homes with paintings. They also donated artistic works to their churches, including altar-pieces and whole series of paintings depicting a cycle of biblical events.

When the technique of oil painting was brought to Venice from Flanders, there was almost an explosion of painting. In Venetian paintings we often find a lighter, more boisterous touch than in the solid paintings of Florence. These paintings often suggest a great symphony of colors. The Venetians seem not to have been deeply concerned with theory and with conscious notions about the place of the human being in the universe.

54. Around the middle of the 1400s, skilled sailors from Portugal and Italy began to explore the Atlantic, looking for a water route to India. They hoped to spread the gospel and to increase their share in the spice trade.

During the fifteenth century the Iberian peninsula (today's Spain and Portugal) was divided into various kingdoms and principalities. In the far west was the kingdom of Portugal. East of it, in the center of the peninsula, came the kingdom of Castile. The eastern and southern regions were under one crown, which governed Aragon, Valencia, and the Catalan principality around Barcelona. A small kingdom centered around Granada in the south was still under Muslim control.

Thanks to its geographical position, the Iberian peninsula could send explorers, traders, or military forces either toward the Atlantic Ocean in the west or toward the Mediterranean Sea in the south and east. The kingdom of Catalonia in the northeast, and particularly the city of Barcelona, had benefited greatly from Mediterranean trade in the waning centuries of the Middle Ages. The kingdom of Castile had some Atlantic trade, particularly with England and the Low Countries; but its attention was mainly turned inward toward reconquering and colonizing devastated areas recently won back from the Muslims.

The great Atlantic adventure was started by a small kingdom which had lain quietly on the margin of Europe: Portugal. The guiding spirit was its ruler, known as Henry the Navigator (1394–1460). Not a navigator himself, he encouraged the collection of geographical and sailing information and founded a school for navigators in Portugal. Skilled Italian sailors and learned geographers joined the newly active Portuguese to achieve a string of brave accomplishments.

The idea of leading a new crusade against Islam was combined with earnest wishes to spread the gospel message. It seemed possible to get around the Turks and link up with isolated Christians in a wealthy Asian kingdom

ruled by a Nestorian Christian known as Prester John. (Today we know that Prester John was only a legendary king, but there really were colonies of Nestorian Christians in Asia.) Sea voyages might also bring new geographical knowledge, open a sea route to the wealth of the Indies in Asia, give Portugal control of the spice trade, and hence have commercial results as well as spiritual benefits.

In the last twenty years of the fifteenth century, finding a sea route to India became a dominant aim of Portugal's exploration policy. Her ships were creeping farther and far-

ther down the African coast. In 1431 the Portuguese had reached the Azores (islands west of Portugal). In 1445 they reached the Cape Verde Islands off the west coast of Africa. In 1482 Diego Cão reached the Congo and part of the coast of what is now Angola. In 1487 Bartholomew Dias rounded the southern tip of Africa, the Cape of Good Hope. He wanted to go on, but his crew insisted on going back home. The way seemed open, though, for future voyages to the Indies and their riches.

55. Around the end of the 1400s, Spain was united under the rule of Ferdinand and Isabella. They completed the reconquest of Spain and drove the Moors from Granada. Isabella and Ferdinand suppressed non-Christian religions, including Judaism and Islam.

In the latter part of the 1400s, two realms of Spain became united under the rule of Isabella and Ferdinand, two sovereigns united by marriage. Isabella was the ruler of Castile, while Ferdinand was the ruler of Aragon and Catalonia and their territories.

One of the major results of this union was the completion of the Reconquest, or the regaining of Spanish lands from the Muslims. Christian colonists had been making their way into the fertile southern plains of Andalusia, held by the Muslims. In 1492 the Muslims of Granada were finally defeated and driven out of Spain. The city of Granada was incorporated into the kingdom of Castile, and its fertile lands became Christian territory. The soldiers, weapons, and monies that had been used for the Reconquest could now be

turned to other uses in Europe, in the Mediterranean region, and far beyond. But the crusading religious mentality of the Reconquest remained alive in Spanish territories, and Spaniards used force to make converts.

Within their realms, Ferdinand and Isabella took charge of much church land and wealth. They strongly supported the Christian religion and the dignity of the papacy, but church affairs in their lands were to be subject to the civil rulers. They, the Catholic Sovereigns of Spain, would reform monastic communities and church life. Fortunately, as we have seen earlier, they chose a great churchman, Cardinal Ximénez de Cisneros, to carry out the reforms, such as stopping the sale of church offices.

Ferdinand and Isabella wanted to suppress non-Christian religions. They forced Jews who would not be baptized to leave Spain. Also, they used the Church's Inquisition to search out, punish, and expel religious dissidents.

The Spanish Inquisition was especially harsh on Muslim Moors and Jews. The Moors of North Africa had invaded Spanish regions centuries ago and conquered the Christian cities and regions. It had taken the Christian Spaniards several centuries to drive the Moors out. This experience with a foreign enemy of a different religion convinced many Spaniards that anyone who was not a Catholic Christian was a potential enemy. They felt that Spain had to put down other religions in order to survive, especially since hostile Muslims remained nearby in North Africa.

The Spanish Inquisition acted against Muslims, Jews, and the few heretics in Spain. Today, the injustice and cruelty of the Inquisition is condemned, but in those days, it was generally accepted as a standard part of a strong government.

56. Christopher Columbus, an Italian sea captain, convinced Queen Isabella to finance his voyage of exploration for a water route to India. Columbus had a strong Christian motive for his voyage. In October, 1492, he reached the shores of a region later known as the Americas. But Columbus thought that he had reached India.

The Portuguese kept looking for a water route to Asia by sailing south and then east along the coast of Africa. Many people now knew that the earth is round and that one therefore should be able to reach the Far East by sailing west across the Atlantic. They felt that their navigators and ships were equal to the task. But they failed to realize how difficult the Atlantic winds and currents were,

and they had no idea that the Americas lay between Europe and Asia.

A Genoese master mariner, Christopher Columbus, who had served in the Portuguese merchant navy, had the courage and persistence to sail across the Atlantic. He called his project "the Enterprise of the Indies," since he hoped to reach India.

Columbus tried unsuccessfully to get backing from the rulers of Portugal, France, and England. Finally Queen Isabella of Castile in Spain gave him three ships, and on August 3, 1492, Columbus sailed from the port of Palos, Spain. The *Niña, Pinta,* and *Santa María* were good ships for their day, but they were quite fragile for such a voyage. The largest, the *Santa María,* was only about seventy-two feet long.

The voyage took more than two months. There were fear, hardship, and a minor mutiny. Then on October 12, 1492, Columbus's ship touched shore. He was greeted with wonder and amazement by the inhabitants of this land. Columbus was convinced—and believed so until his death—that he had reached the eastern tip of the continent of Asia and that the fabulous Indies lay before him. In fact, he had reached one of the islands of the Bahamas and a whole new continental area, the Americas.

Columbus, a devout Christian, always felt that his explorations were opening up new areas where the Christian faith could flourish. Since the Bible mentions only Africa and Eurasia, he could not believe that other continents existed. When subsequent voyages did not bring him the rich treasures he had expected to find, he preferred to think that he had touched the banks of the heavenly Paradise.

Columbus brought back to Europe some unknown animals, modest amounts of gold, and some native Americans, to whom he gave the name "Indians." In his last years he faced misfortune and imprisonment. In 1506 he died neglected and almost forgotten.

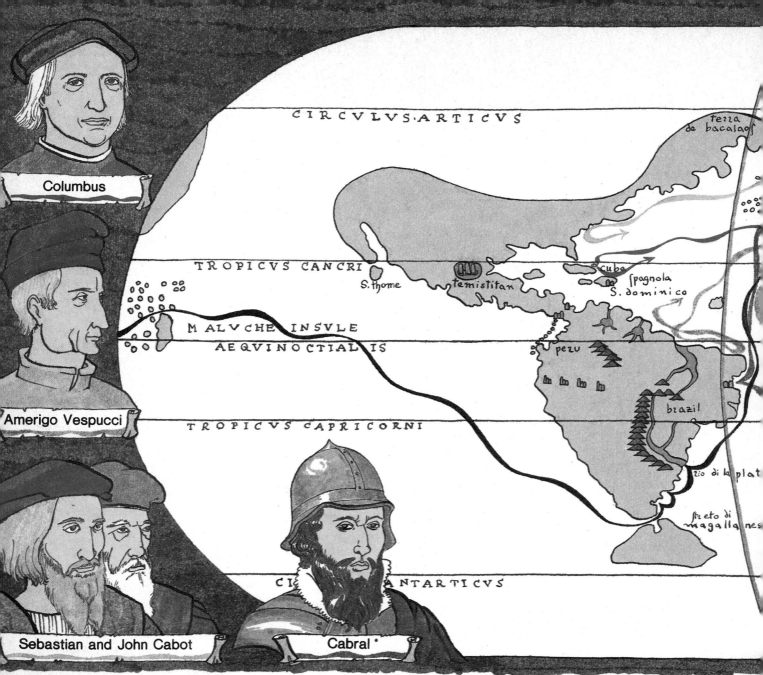

57. The search for wealth
and precious goods
urged sailors and explorers
of Spain and Portugal
on to new discoveries.
A treaty signed between
the two countries stated
how the newly-discovered
lands were to be divided
between them. They did
not seem to consider
that the lands belonged
to the people living there.

Further voyages convinced people that the lands discovered by Columbus were not part of the Asian continent. New explorers and conquerors hastened over to win gold and riches for themselves. Rivalry broke out between Spain and Portugal, and it threatened to lead to war over any new discoveries. Thanks to the intervention of Pope Alexander VI, Spain and Portugal signed the Treaty of Tordesillas in 1494. Isabella and her successors were given a right to all non-Christian lands west of a line drawn from pole to pole 360 leagues west of the Cape Verde Islands. The Portuguese king had the same right to lands to the east. The European rulers did not seem to consider that these lands belonged to the people who lived there.

In 1497–1498 the Portuguese sailor Vasco da Gama rounded the Cape of Good Hope, sailed up the eastern coast of Africa, and then made his way safely to Calcutta, India. The water route to India had been found! In 1500

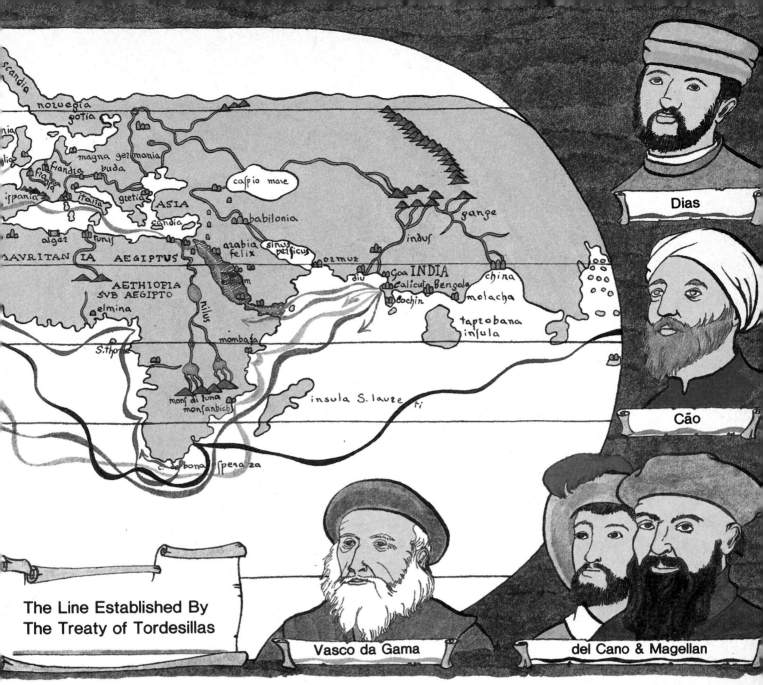

The Line Established By
The Treaty of Tordesillas

Dias

Cão

Vasco da Gama

del Cano & Magellan

another Portuguese captain, Pedro Alvares Cabral, went off course while rounding Africa and ended up in Brazil. This newly-discovered territory fell on Portugal's side of the line established by the Treaty of Tordesillas.

Meanwhile the Spanish were not idle. They had begun settlements in Central America, along the isthmus coast which Columbus had found on his fourth voyage. In 1513 Vasco Núñez de Balboa crossed the isthmus between North and South America and reached the shores of the Pacific Ocean. They looked for a strait through the land, because then one could find a westward sea-route to the East after all! Searches farther north proved fruitless. The search farther south was successful in 1522 when a single ship with eighteen men straggled into port after a three-year voyage. It was the surviving remnant of an expedition which had set out under Castilian auspices and a Portuguese captain, Ferdinand Magellan. He had died in the Philippines, but his

expedition had sailed west around the globe and ended up back home in Europe, under the command of Captain del Cano.

Many other famous explorers made important discoveries during this time. Among them were John Cabot, who reached the North American continent, and his son Sebastian, who reached Hudson Bay. Amerigo Vespucci is remembered especially by Americans because he gave his name to their continents. The pictures of these and other explorers are placed around the picture of an ancient map showing the division of the newly-found lands. (It would be interesting and fun to compare this map with a modern map of the world.)

Ahead lay conquests and colonies, profitable trade and exploration. Ahead lay new fields for preaching the gospel message. Ahead, too, lay meetings with different peoples and cultures on which Europeans would sometimes have a devastating effect.

58. The kingdom of the Congo in Africa was reached by the Portuguese in 1482. A little later, friendly relations were established between Congo and Europe under the rule of Affonso I, a Christian Congo king.

But then Europeans began to steal people from the Congo and sell them as slaves. Slave trade grew rapidly, bringing great suffering to the people of Africa.

In 1482 the Portuguese captain Diego Cão came upon the large, well organized kingdom of the Congo (or Kongo). It was part of the Bantu-speaking region of Africa, on a plateau south of the Congo River. Its king was an absolute, semi-divine monarch, governing right down to the village level.

Early relations were friendly. On various trips Diego Cão brought missionaries to the Congo and Congo nobles back to Portugal. The king, Nzinga Kuvu, was baptized in 1491, along with other members of his family. Most of them soon abandoned Christianity. But one man did not. He fought a non-Christian relative for the throne and came to rule as King Affonso I. He planned to bring great progress to his people through Christianity and contacts with Portugal.

Affonso encouraged the work of missionaries and the buildup of the Church. Many of his people became Christians and were educated by Portuguese priests. Some from noble Congo families went to Portugal for advanced education. In 1518 one son of Affonso was consecrated a bishop in Rome. Another son remained in Lisbon to teach the humanities. Affonso himself, as a Christian prince, had already vowed his obedience to the pope in 1513.

Affonso saw himself as an equal of the King of Portugal, a brother monarch, and he seems to have been accepted as such by the latter. He paid for the services of the Portuguese by sending iron, copper, and slaves to Portugal.

The slave trade was already active in Africa, and all too quickly Europeans were drawn to it. They would deal with African slave merchants, capture prisoners, and even kidnap unprotected African children playing along the shores of the African coast. King Affonso's dream of progress and friendly relations in his own kingdom was undermined by growing greed for gold, profits, and slaves among his native vassals and his Portuguese fellow-Christians.

As early as 1526 Affonso had complained to King John of Portugal that Portuguese officials and merchants were stealing his subjects and selling them. He wanted some priests and a few teachers for his schools. And he wanted an end to the slave trade.

Unfortunately, even some priests got used to owning slaves and trading in them. Relations worsened. Affonso was nearly assassinated by some Portuguese in 1539. There is no record of his death, but he ranks as one of the truly pioneering rulers in the history of Africa.

59. For many centuries, people had believed that the earth was the center of the universe and that the planets and the sun moved around it. This idea was supported, they thought, by the Bible and by the theories of Ptolemy. But around the year 1450, Nicholas Copernicus, a Polish priest, claimed that the earth and all the planets revolved around the sun.

The period of history (1250–1650) covered in this volume and the next one was a time of transition in Europe. To many people, 1250 to 1450 was a period of decay and death—the "autumn" of the Middle Ages, as historian John Huizinga put it. But it was also a time of planting seeds that bore fruit during the next two hundred years. From 1450 to 1650 a new Europe clearly emerged; by 1650 or 1700 the foundations of a more modern world had been laid. There were sudden spurts and retreats here and there, but all in all the change was slow and gradual.

The way modern science slowly developed out of ancient and medieval roots is a good example of that process of change. As time went on, scientists began to observe the world about them more closely. They combined that close observation with new theories, deductions (lines of reasoning), and mathematical calculations.

A Polish priest named Nicholas Copernicus illustrates how modern science (and hence the modern world) was slowly developing. Copernicus studied in Italy between 1496 and 1506. While there, he pondered the accepted Ptolemaic view of the universe: a motionless earth at the center of the universe, with the sun, moon, and planets revolving around it. But Copernicus thought it unlikely that such a

large body as the sun would revolve around a smaller body, the earth. And he knew that Aristarchus, an ancient Greek astronomer, had argued that the earth and all planets revolved around the sun, and that the earth also turned on its axis.

Copernicus decided to use mathematical calculations to see which theory offered better results. He concluded that a more probable and simpler system resulted if one assumed that the sun, not the earth, was the center of the system. Copernicus' theory of the sun as the center of the universe explained such things as the variations of the seasons, and the apparent movements of planets observed from earth. He presented his theory in his major work, *On the Revolutions of the Heavenly Spheres,* which was published shortly after his death in 1543.

Copernicus did not solve all his problems or fully prove his theory, so there was still room for reasonable scientific doubt. But many theologians reacted strongly against the theory on biblical grounds, because the Bible referred to the sun's moving. But by the end of the sixteenth century the Copernican theory had been given solid support by the work of such people as Johannes Kepler and Galileo Galilei. By the end of the seventeenth century this new view of the universe and its workings had been further explained by Isaac Newton. This centuries-long process of scientific development is a good example of the major transition through which Europe was going, leading toward the modern world.

Outline by Chapter

The Church in the Age of Humanism

Note to Readers: The *c.* before some dates is an abbreviation for *circa*, meaning "about" or "approximately."